LINGUISTIC RELATIVITY TODAY

This is the first textbook on the linguistic relativity hypothesis, presenting it in user-friendly language, yet analyzing all its premises in systematic ways. The hypothesis claims that there is an intrinsic interconnection between thought, language, and society. All technical terms are explained and a glossary is provided at the back of the volume. The book looks at the history and different versions of the hypothesis over the centuries, including the research paradigms and critiques that it has generated. It also describes and analyzes the relevant research designed to test its validity in various domains of language structure and use, from grammar and discourse to artificial languages and in nonverbal semiotic systems as well. Overall, this book aims to present a comprehensive overview of the hypothesis and its supporting research in a textbook fashion, with pedagogical activities in each chapter, including questions for discussion and practical exercises on specific notions associated with the hypothesis. The book also discusses the hypothesis as a foundational notion for the establishment of linguistic anthropology as a major branch of linguistics. This essential course text inspires creative, informed dialogue and debate for students of anthropology, linguistics, cultural studies, cognitive science, and psychology.

Marcel Danesi is Full Professor of Linguistic Anthropology at the University of Toronto. He has written extensively on linguistic and semiotic topics, and was distinguished for his research by the Canadian government with a Fellowship of the Royal Society of Canada.

Routledge Foundations in Linguistic Anthropology

Books in the **Routledge Foundations in Linguistic Anthropology** series serve as frameworks for courses on the sub-areas of Linguistic Anthropology. Each book concisely lays out the groundwork for instructors to introduce students to these topics, and are structured in a way that enables the use of additional readings and resources to tailor each course. Serving as great jumping-off points for discussion, these books are ideal for undergraduate- and graduate-level Linguistic Anthropology courses.

Food and Language
Discourses and Foodways across Cultures
Kathleen C. Riley and Amy L. Paugh

Linguistic Relativity Today
Language, Mind, Society, and the Foundations of Linguistic Anthropology
Marcel Danesi

For more information about this series, please visit:
https://www.routledge.com/Routledge-Foundations-in-Linguistic-Anthropology/book-series/RFLA

LINGUISTIC RELATIVITY TODAY

Language, Mind, Society, and the Foundations of Linguistic Anthropology

Marcel Danesi

NEW YORK AND LONDON

First published 2021
by Routledge
52 Vanderbilt Avenue, New York, NY 10017

and by Routledge
2 Park Square, Milton Park, Abingdon, Oxon, OX14 4RN

Routledge is an imprint of the Taylor & Francis Group, an informa business

© 2021 Taylor & Francis

The right of Marcel Danesi to be identified as author of this work has been asserted by him in accordance with sections 77 and 78 of the Copyright, Designs and Patents Act 1988.

All rights reserved. No part of this book may be reprinted or reproduced or utilised in any form or by any electronic, mechanical, or other means, now known or hereafter invented, including photocopying and recording, or in any information storage or retrieval system, without permission in writing from the publishers.

Trademark notice: Product or corporate names may be trademarks or registered trademarks, and are used only for identification and explanation without intent to infringe.

Library of Congress Cataloging-in-Publication Data
Names: Danesi, Marcel, 1946- author.
Title: Linguistic relativity today : language, mind, society, and the foundations of linguistic anthropology / Marcel Danesi.
Description: New York : Routledge, 2021. | Series: Routledge foundations in linguistic anthropology | Includes bibliographical references and index.
Identifiers: LCCN 2020040817 (print) | LCCN 2020040818 (ebook) | ISBN 9780367431723 (paperback) | ISBN 9780367431730 (hardback) | ISBN 9781003001669 (ebook)
Subjects: LCSH: Linguistic anthropology. | Language and culture.
Classification: LCC P35 .D36 2021 (print) | LCC P35 (ebook) | DDC 306.44--dc23
LC record available at https://lccn.loc.gov/2020040817
LC ebook record available at https://lccn.loc.gov/2020040818

ISBN: 978-0-367-43173-0 (hbk)
ISBN: 978-0-367-43172-3 (pbk)
ISBN: 978-1-003-00166-9 (ebk)

Typeset in Times New Roman
by SPi Global, India

CONTENTS

Preface	viii
List of Abbreviations	xi

1	Overview	1
	Prologue	1
	Background	3
	Linguistic Anthropology	8
	Linguistic Relativity	9
	Investigating Linguistic Relativity	13
	Critiques	15
	Epilogue	18
	Discussion Questions and Activities	20

2	Early Research on Linguistic Relativity	22
	Prologue	22
	Franz Boas and Edward Sapir	23
	Lev S. Vygotsky	28
	Relevant Research Questions	31
	Epilogue	36
	Discussion Questions and Activities	37

3	The Whorfian Hypothesis	40
	Prologue	40
	The Hopi Language	41
	Critical Reactions	44
	Resurgence of Interest	47
	Sound Symbolism	51
	Epilogue	53
	Discussion Questions and Activities	55
4	Vocabulary and Grammar	58
	Prologue	58
	Specialized Vocabulary	59
	Kinship Terms	62
	Color Terms	63
	Grammar	70
	Habitual Thought	73
	Epilogue	75
	Discussion Questions and Activities	77
5	Discourse and Translation	79
	Prologue	79
	Discursive Relativity	80
	Translation	85
	Machine Translation	91
	Epilogue	94
	Discussion Questions and Activities	95
6	Figurative Language	98
	Prologue	98
	Conceptual Metaphor Theory	100
	Idealized Cognitive Models	105
	Extensions	109
	Epilogue	113
	Discussion Questions and Activities	115
7	Computer-Mediated Communication, AI, and Artificial Languages	118
	Prologue	118
	Computer-Mediated Communication	119
	Artificial Intelligence	122
	Artificial Languages	125

Epilogue	127
Implications of Linguistic Relativity	128
Concluding Remarks	130
Discussion Questions and Activities	131
Glossary	134
References	139
Index	156

PREFACE

In a 1921 volume entitled *Language: An introduction to the study of speech*, which became a founding text in early twentieth-century linguistics, Edward Sapir argued persuasively that the words and grammatical categories of the language (or languages) we acquire in childhood will affect and shape our subsequent thoughts and filter our experiences, rather than simply encode them. Sapir never designed and carried out an empirical research program aimed at examining his argument systematically. The onus of researching it fell on the shoulders of his own student, Benjamin Lee Whorf (1956), who studied with Sapir in the early 1930s. At the time, Sapir himself had somewhat abandoned his idea, but Whorf saw it as immensely intriguing. Encouraged nonetheless by his teacher, Whorf conducted extensive fieldwork on Sapir's original idea among the speakers of Native American languages, focusing on the Hopi language spoken in north-eastern Arizona. From his research, he concluded that the particular native language we learn in socio-cultural context influences how we think, act, and behave, both as individuals and as entire societies (groupthink). He named this synergy between language, mind, society, and culture *linguistic relativity*. The word *hypothesis*—in the term *linguistic relativity hypothesis* (LRH)—was added after Whorf died in 1941. The LRH became broadly accepted among linguists, leading to extensive research on it shortly thereafter, encompassing many languages. The accumulated data on the LRH is now quite extensive and convincing overall, even though it has been the target of often heated debate and controversy since at least the middle part of the 1960s. Whether one espouses it or not, there is little doubt that it remains a fascinating and important idea for linguists, psychologists, anthropologists, and even computer scientists to investigate.

I have been teaching linguistics since 1972, and have always incorporated the LRH into my classes. I have done so through handouts and my own exercise materials since, to this day, there is no introductory non-technical textbook on the LRH. This led to my decision to compile such a book, since I believe that the LRH is one of the most interesting themes in linguistics, as students have consistently told me over the years. This text can hopefully be useful in courses in introductory linguistics, psychology, or anthropology, either as a supplementary or complementary manual. My overall objective has been to provide a general assessment of the significance of the LRH to the study of the language–thought–culture-society nexus, reviewing the main findings and discussing them in non-technical ways. Whorf was aware that the LRH would raise questions connected to its definition, since terms such as *thinking* or *thought*, are much too vague. So, he assumed that everyone would understand what they meant intuitively, focusing instead on examining how *thinking* is built into in the grammatical categories and vocabulary systems of different languages, which not only can be studied precisely, but can also be used to extract relevant insights on the language-thought nexus. He put it thus (Whorf 1965: 252):

> Thinking is most mysterious, and by far the greatest light upon it that we have is thrown by the study of language. This study shows that the forms of a person's thoughts are controlled by inexorable laws of pattern of which he is unconscious. These patterns are the unperceived intricate systematizations of his own language—shown readily enough by a candid comparison and contrast with other languages, especially those of a different linguistic family. His thinking itself is in a language—in English, in Sanskrit, in Chinese. And every language is a vast pattern-system, different from others, in which are culturally ordained the forms and categories by which the personality not only communicates, but also analyzes nature, notices or neglects types of relationship and phenomena, channels his reasoning, and builds the house of his consciousness.

Sapir himself was a pupil of anthropologist-linguist Franz Boas at Columbia University in the first decade of the twentieth century. Boas was among the first American linguists to focus concretely on the relation between language structures, society, thought, and culture—a focus that became the founding principle of what came to be called *anthropological linguistics*, known more commonly today as *linguistic anthropology*. The early linguists, inspired by Boas and Sapir, carried out extensive fieldwork on the relation between the indigenous languages and cultures of North America, guided in large part by what eventually came to be known as the LRH. With the advent of generative grammar in the late 1950s as a mainstream movement, this line of inquiry was temporarily marginalized. However, by the mid-1980s interest in studying the LRH was reignited as a new orientation in linguistics, called *cognitive linguistics,* came forward to provide new ways to study its manifestations.

The fundamental question raised by the LRH is whether people who speak different languages also think differently; and if so, how so or to what degree. From the relevant studies, there is little support for the so-called "strong" version—namely, the claim that language *determines* how people think, known more specifically as *linguistic determinism*. However, the research strongly suggests that thinking is indeed shaped by the particular language (or languages) one has learned in childhood. Incidentally, Whorf never espoused linguistic determinism, even though he was accused of doing so. His term, *linguistic relativity,* was actually meant to reject determinism, suggesting an intrinsic (not deterministic) interrelationship between language and thought.

This book looks comprehensively at the LRH, from its historical genesis to the kinds of research questions it raises today for the evolution of language in the age of the Internet. I have written it in user-friendly style, making no assumptions with regard to technical terms and concepts on the part of the reader. Each chapter starts with a prologue that presents anecdotal situations eliciting questions that are used to introduce the main themes of the chapter. Information on technical terms, ideas, and so on are included in boxes throughout, so that the reader does not have to search for them elsewhere when they come up in the discussion. At the end of each chapter, there are two pedagogically-relevant sections: *Discussion Questions* and *Activities*. A *Glossary* of key terms is provided at the back of the book.

I must inform the reader that I have had to be selective about what to treat and what not to treat, given the enormity of the research on the LRH, although I have attempted to cast as wide a net as possible. I should also mention that I have rephrased or simplified some notions in order to make them understandable to the non-expert. I sincerely hope that this text will pique the interests of students, or anyone else, to investigate the language–society–thought–culture nexus on their own. The suggestions and commentaries that my own students have passed on to me over the decades have guided every stage in the preparation of this book. I feel truly fortunate and privileged to have had the opportunity to share my views with so many over the years. I thank one and all from the bottom of my heart. Their enthusiasm has always made my job as a teacher simply wonderful. I dedicate this book to them.

ABBREVIATIONS

AGI	artificial general intelligence
AI	artificial intelligence
CMC	computer-mediated communication
CMT	conceptual metaphor theory
FL	foreign language
GP	grammatical programming
HDTP	heuristic-driven theory projection
HMC	human–machine communication
ICM	idealized cognitive model
LP	lexical programming
LRH	linguistic relativity hypothesis
MT	machine translation
NL	native language
NLP	natural language programming
SAE	Standard Average European
SL	source language
SVO	subject–verb–object
TL	target language
UG	Universal Grammar
WH	Whorfian hypothesis

1
OVERVIEW

Prologue

An anecdote is told about the Polish-American scholar Alfred Korzybski (cited in Derks and Hollander 1996: 58), who founded an interdisciplinary field called *general semantics* in order to study how knowledge and linguistic habits of mind are constrained by the nervous system (Korzybski 1921, 1933). It is reported that one day, as he was giving a lecture to a group of students, he suddenly stopped talking to retrieve a packet of biscuits from his briefcase, telling the class that he was very hungry and needed to eat something right away. He then asked several students in the front row if they would also like a biscuit. A few took one, eating in front of him, after which Korzybski asked, "Nice biscuit, don't you think?" He then ripped off the white paper wrapper around the packet, revealing the picture of a dog's head and the tagline *Dog Cookies*. The students who had just eaten the biscuits became visibly upset by this revelation, and a few put a hand in front of their mouths as they ran to the toilets. Korzybski then remarked to the rest of the class: "You see, I have just demonstrated that people don't just eat food, but also words, and that the taste of the former is often outdone by the taste of the latter."

This anecdote encapsulates what the subject matter of this book is essentially about, and the type of questions it will attempt to address: Do words affect how we perceive things and influence how we react physically and emotionally? Does the particular native language we learned in childhood shape how we understand the world? Can we think without words? If so, what would thought be like without them? Korzybski's little mind game was designed to bring out the intrinsic relation that exists between language, thought, and behavior in a nutshell. The formal study of this relation comes under the rubric of the linguistic relativity hypothesis (LRH). A fundamental tenet of this hypothesis is, in fact, that words are not merely arbitrary labels for things; rather, they influence how we think, act, and react. Let us repeat Korzybski's experiment hypothetically using another illustrative word game. Suppose that this time we prepared a meal consisting of little meat-like pieces for another class of North American students, which they seemingly eat gladly with no adverse reactions. After the meal, we tell them that they had just eaten *silkworms*. What would their probable reaction be now? It is likely that most would react negatively, as did the students who ate the dog biscuits. However, the same word in Spanish, *gusano de seda*, would hardly produce this reaction in Mexicans who live in the central valleys of Oaxaca, because they eat cooked silkworms as a delicacy. Again, the negative reaction on the part of our (hypothetical) students had nothing to do with the substance or quality of the meal but with the coded (culture-specific) meanings that the word *silkworm* evoked.

Discussions and debates on the LRH are replete with anecdotal examples such as these. But is there any empirical support? One of the central aims of this book is to look at relevant studies that have examined the LRH empirically. The objective of this opening chapter is to provide an overview of the origins and underlying premises of the hypothesis, including how it is defined, how it is broken down linguistically and psychologically, and what main critiques have been leveled against it. As we shall see, a common approach to investigating the LRH is comparing specific grammatical and lexical structures of different languages. For instance, in English, the device that marks the passage of time is named a *watch*, if it is portable or wearable on the human body, usually on the wrist, but a *clock*, if it is to be put somewhere as, for example, on a table, or on a wall. In Italian, no such conceptual distinction has been encoded lexically. There is only one word in that language, *orologio*, for designating any device for keeping track of time, wearable or not. This does not mean that Italian does not have the linguistic resources for making the same distinction marked in English by two words, if needed. The phrasal structure *da* ("at") + *place* allows Italian speakers to provide the same kind of conceptual differentiation: *orologio da polso* ("wrist watch"), *orologio da muro* ("wall clock"), and so on. But in practice this distinction is not marked overtly in Italian when the topic of time-keeping devices comes up in discourse. Now, the relevant question is: Does the fact that speakers of English and Italian have different ways of referring to time-keeping devices signal a different perception of time in the two cultures? If so, how so?

The study of time as a cultural construct led, actually, to the establishment of a subfield of anthropology in 1967 by E. P. Thompson, who argued that the observance of clock-time emerged during the Industrial Revolution in the nineteenth century, leading to labor practices and behavioral interactions governed by precision in time-keeping—hence the need for clocks and watches. Events that seem so "natural" to us today, such as arranging meetings at specific times, would be literally unthinkable without this nineteenth-century construct. One of the goals of LRH-based research has been, actually, to investigate whether the linguistic categories related to time, such as verb tenses, influence the perception of time in speakers of different languages—a topic that will be discussed in due course.

The Korzybski anecdote bears much more significance than what it might seem at first. It describes in microcosm the kind of experiment that has actually been conducted by linguists and psychologists to test the validity of the LRH, as we shall see. It is also the kind of mind game that has come under acerbic criticism by those who see the LRH as meaningless. Whatever the truth, the LRH is still one of the most interesting ideas in contemporary linguistics, even if it turns out to be nothing more than speculation. This chapter looks at the historical background to the hypothesis and what it has meant for the evolution of linguistics as a science of language. It is based on three questions, which are repeated in the discussion section at the end of this chapter, as part of its pedagogical objectives:

1. What is the notion of linguistic relativity?
2. What are its origins?
3. Is it relevant or useful to understanding the role of language in human life?

Background

The LRH has focused, by and large, on addressing two fundamental questions: Does the particular native language one speaks habitually influence the thoughts a speaker has? Does a specific language affect how its speakers understand reality, known as *worldview*? To investigate these questions in any meaningful way, a viable theory or model of language is required. In contemporary linguistics, the term *grammar* is understood (generically) as the system of structural units of a language and the rules for constructing and combining them—it is clearly an important concept in the study of the LRH. The Indian scholar Pāṇini, who lived around the fifth century BCE, was among the first to conduct a scientific analysis of a particular grammar—the grammar of the Sanskrit language. Pāṇini described its minimal units, now called *morphemes*, in great detail, relating them to how they formed more complex structures with rules of combination, called the *syntax*. He also showed that the grammar and the lexicon of Sanskrit—the set of items, now called *lexemes*, that bear meaning in themselves—were interactive components.

> **MORPHEMES AND LEXEMES**
>
> *Morpheme:* a meaning-bearing unit of language that cannot be subdivided further. In English, for example, the word *incompletely* is made up of three morphemes: *in* + *complete* + *ly*. Two of them (*in-* and *-ly*) recur in the formation of other words and are thus considered to be units in the grammar of English, known as *affixes*; on the other hand, *complete* has lexical (dictionary) meaning, and is thus part of the lexicon of English.
>
> *Lexeme:* a unit that has lexical meaning, such as *complete* above. Other examples are: *love* in *lovely*, *spread* in *spreading*, *live* in *relive*, and so on.
>
> *Morphology:* the formal study of word-construction in terms of morphemes and how they are combined; the study of *lexemes* falls more directly under *lexicology* (the study of lexical categories) and *semantics* (the study of the meaning patterns of lexemes and their uses).
>
> *Syntax:* the study of the rules of arrangement of the morphemes and lexemes of a language for constructing complex structures such as phrases and sentences.

Pāṇini identified about 4,000 *sutras*, in his treatise, the *Ashtadhyayi*. These are the morphemes and the rules of syntax for combining them into complex structures (Kadvany 2007). He also introduced the notion of mapping, prefiguring current models of language, whereby one set of *sutras* are mapped onto other grammatical domains (including other *sutras*) to produce a complete grammar (Prince and Smolensky 2004).

The birth of linguistics as the science of language is traced to the discovery and translation of Pāṇini's pioneering work by European philologists in the nineteenth century. It influenced the founder of modern linguistics, the Swiss philologist Ferdinand de Saussure (1916), who was himself a professor of Sanskrit (discussed below). Pāṇini's grammar provided a model of language that made it possible to raise a series of specific questions that related to the LRH, although not named at the time as such. For example, do languages that form their sentences with words consisting of clusters of morphemes, known as *agglutinative* languages, shape the thoughts of speakers differentially from the thoughts of speakers of languages that depend largely on word order, or syntax, known as *isolating* languages (Greenberg 1966)?

> **TYPES OF LANGUAGES**
>
> *Agglutinative:* languages characterized by words generally made up of more than one morpheme; that is, one word = several morphemes. An example of an agglutinative language is Wishram, a variant of Chinook (a North American

Native Language), in which the word *ačimluda* ("He will give it to you"), for example, is composed of the morphemes /a-/ indicating the future tense, /-č-/ standing for the pronoun "he," /-i-/ "it," /-m-/ "you," /-l-/ "to," /-ud-/ "give," and again /-a/ future tense.

Inflectional/Fusional: languages in which a single morpheme stands for multiple meanings or grammatical functions. For example, the preterite form of the French verb *parler* ("to speak"), (*il*) *parla* ("he spoke"), is constructed with the single suffix morpheme /-a/, which represents both the third-person singular subject and the preterite tense, instead of having a separate morpheme for each.

Synthetic: languages that use inflection or agglutination to establish grammatical relationships within sentences, or to change the grammatical category to which a word belongs. For instance, adding /-ment/ to the verb *govern* produces the noun *government*; adding /-er/ to the adjective *quick* produces the comparative form *quicker*; and so on.

Isolating/Analytic: languages that convey meaning by rules of word order (syntax). For example, the English sentence "*The dog bit the cat*" conveys the fact that the dog is acting on the cat through word order. Changing the order, changes the meaning: "*The cat bit the dog.*"

Note: There is no language that is exclusively agglutinative, isolating, and so on. It is a matter of degree. For instance, English is largely an isolating language, but it also has many agglutinative, synthetic, and fusional aspects in its grammar.

Employing such typological categories, the early twentieth-century linguist, Edward Sapir (1921), became an early pioneer in discussing the implications of the LRH, although he never identified it as such—the term *linguistic relativity* was put forth by Benjamin Lee Whorf (Sapir's own student) a little later, in analogy with the physical theory of relativity (Whorf 1940: 229): "We are thus introduced to a new principle of relativity, which holds that all observers are not led by the same physical evidence to the same picture of the universe, unless their linguistic backgrounds are similar, or can in some way be calibrated." Without going into details at this point, suffice it to say that Sapir saw an intrinsic linkage between language type (agglutinative, isolating, and so on) and differences in thinking exhibited by speakers of the different types.

The belief that language and thought are linked in some way is actually an ancient one; it was encapsulated in ancient Greece by the term *lógos* (λόγος). In his book on *Rhetoric*, Aristotle (1952a) saw *lógos* as the use of words to articulate a logical argument (Dineen 1995; Law 2003). He was also the first to identify the two main parts of a sentence as intrinsic components of grammar, calling them the *subject* and the *predicate.* A couple of centuries later, the scholar Dionysius Thrax, who lived between 170 and 90 BCE, named the parts of speech that constitute sentences as *nouns, verbs, articles, pronouns, prepositions, conjunctions, adverbs,* and *participles* (Robins 1967; Seuren 1998). The Roman Priscian, who lived in the sixth century CE, applied this model to Latin grammar—a model that was adopted by Europeans in the fourteenth and fifteenth centuries for writing the grammars of their own languages, even if the fit was not always perfect (Robins 1967). The key aspect of this approach was the premise that the specific words in sentences are not put together in a haphazard order, but, rather, by rules of arrangement of the parts of speech.

This premise was examined further by a group of French scholars in the seventeenth century, who came to be known as members of the Port-Royal Circle. In their 1660 book, *Grammaire générale et raisonnée contenant les fondemens de l'art de parler, expliqués d'une manière claire et naturelle* ("General and Rational Grammar, Containing the Fundamentals of the Art of Speaking, Explained in a Clear and Natural Manner"), now known generally as the *Port-Royal Grammar*, Antoine Arnauld and Claude Lancelot—two leading members of the Circle—put forth the notion that the manner in which the parts of speech were organized in the sentences of all languages of the world, no matter how different, followed the same rules of syntax, with variations, because they were part of a universal mental process (Rieux and Rollin 1975). The details varied from language to language, but the rule types did not.

By the middle part of the nineteenth century, such ideas were debated concretely, as philologists studied common features, which they even called laws, of how languages changed over time, laying the groundwork for a science of language to emerge. It was Saussure (1916), as mentioned above, who put the finishing touches to this fledgling science, which he called *linguistique* ("linguistics"), by making a distinction between the study of how languages changed, which he called *diachronic*, and the systematic study of a language at a specific point in time, which he called *synchronic*. He also proposed (in synch with the Port-Royal grammarians) that linguistics should focus on examining the universal structure of language, which he called *langue* ("language"), rather than on *parole* ("word"), or the use of language in speech. Saussure also argued that the signs used in a language, such as single words, are arbitrary referential structures. So, for instance, the word *tree* in English and *arbre* in French referred to the same concept ("arboreal plant")—only the linguistic labels differed. Saussure's view implied that speakers of different languages had the "same picture of the universe," not a different one (as Whorf suggested above). Hence, the Saussurean approach was one of the first implicit arguments within linguistics against the LRH.

His view was contested indirectly by the German-born American anthropologist Franz Boas in the early part of the twentieth century (Boas 1911), who showed that there were indeed different pictures of the universe in the minds of the speakers of different languages. By collecting extensive data on the Native languages of North America, Boas aimed to show how their grammars and lexicons reflected different cultural emphases, which in turn involved different worldviews. At around the same time, British anthropologist Evans-Pritchard (1940) provided supporting evidence for this perspective, with his work on the culture and language spoken by the Nuer, a herding people of eastern Africa. For example, he found that there are many words in that language for the colors and markings of cattle, and the reason for this was the importance of livestock in that culture. In English, on the other hand, there are very few words for livestock, but many for describing music (*classical, jazz, folk, rock*, etc.), revealing instead the importance of music in Western society. It was this kind of "relativistic" approach to language that laid the groundwork for anthropological linguistics to emerge as an autonomous field focusing on a supposed language-mind-culture-society nexus.

For decades subsequent to Boas, linguists went about the painstaking work of documenting how different languages mirrored different cultural emphases and perceptions of reality. The first major break with this tradition came in 1957, when the American linguist Noam Chomsky argued that an understanding of language as a universal faculty of the brain could never be developed from a piecemeal description of the disparate structures of widely divergent languages. Reviving the views of the Port-Royal grammarians and Saussure, Chomsky claimed that a true theory of language would have to explain why all languages reveal a similar structural plan for constructing their grammars. The specific rules of the grammar of a certain language are based on that plan, which was eventually called Universal Grammar (UG). The UG would purportedly explain why children learn to speak so naturally, without training of any kind (Chomsky 1975). All that is needed is exposure to samples of a language and the child will easily construct the grammar from them, guided by the UG in the brain. Differences in language grammars are due to choices of rule types, called parameters, from the UG. Without going into the debates on UG here, a major problem with this model is that it ignores a fundamental creative force in early infancy—the ability to make imitative linguistic models of actions and events in the world, and to invent expressions based on inferences and analogies to fill in gaps of knowledge (Crystal 1987: 232). For example, when children lack a word for the concept of *moon*, they may come up with a metaphorical strategy, such as calling it a *ball*, which they had previously learned, indicating that they envision a similarity of shape between the two referents, classifying them ("moon" and "ball") as a unitary concept with the same linguistic label. Only when children learn the word *moon* as a distinctive sign in context do they develop different conceptualizations of "ball" and "moon."

Linguistic Anthropology

Boas founded anthropological linguistics at Columbia University in 1899, developing research methods that made it possible for the first time to study linguistic relativity meaningfully (Boas 1920). One of these methods was fieldwork, whereby the linguist would live and interact among those who speak a specific language, gathering information from them in order to understand what the functions of the language are, and how they differed from the native language of the field worker. The language Boas himself chose to study in detail was that of the Kwakiutl, a native society on the north-western coast of North America. In what is now a classic book in anthropological linguistics, *Race, Language, and Culture* (1940), a collection of his papers published between 1887 and 1937, Boas documented how the grammar and lexicon of the Kwakiutl language reflected their differential ways of thinking about the world vis-à-vis English speakers. Each lexeme and unit of grammar in Kwakiutl was hardly an arbitrary sign structure; rather it reflected specific modes of thinking that were found in other domains of Kwakiutl society—in symbolism, narratives, rituals, and so on.

The term *linguistic anthropology*, as an alternative to *anthropological linguistics*, was put forth a while later by linguist Dell Hymes (1963), who wanted to broaden the Boasian approach to encompass the study of the strategic uses and functions of language in communicative contexts. To do so concretely, he introduced the notion of *communicative competence* a little later to indicate the kind of social knowledge that shapes how language is used in specific contexts (Hymes 1971). Hymes argued that such knowledge is hardly separate from knowledge of the language itself (known as linguistic competence)—one required the other. Change in language comes from its use, not from any inner evolutionary force. As we speak, from generation to generation, modes of communicating start to vary; as these accumulate over time, they lead to structural changes in the language to accommodate the new modes.

Starting in the mid-1970s, linguists took Hymes' ideas to heart and began studying communicative competence seriously, simultaneously expanding the research paradigm in linguistic anthropology to include such areas of investigation as the construction of interpersonal and social identities through discourse, the manifestation of shared ideologies in conversations, and so on (Duranti 2003; Kulick 1992; Ochs and Schieffelin 1984; Ochs and Taylor 2001; Silverstein 1976, 1979). In the same time frame, an approach to language called *cognitive linguistics* also emerged to explain the influence of figurative language on thought processes (Honeck and Hoffman 1980; Lakoff and Johnson 1980; Ortony 1979; Pollio, Barlow, Fine, and Pollio 1977). The most prominent figure in the first stages of the movement was the American linguist George Lakoff, whose book *Metaphors We Live By* (198), co-authored with Mark Johnson, became a key text in the early period. In his subsequent influential book, *Women, Fire, and Dangerous Things* (Lakoff 1987), Lakoff argued persuasively that the foundations of a language were connected to differing culture-based experiences, recalling Boas' approach. As an illustration, he discussed grammatical gender in the Australian language Dyirbal. In European languages, the gender of a noun referring to inanimate objects is unpredictable from its meaning. For example, the word for "table" is masculine in German (*der Tisch*), feminine in French (*la table*), and neuter in Greek (*to trapézi*). In Dyirbal, however, the gender of a noun is determined from cultural values and emphases—nouns referring to *women* are assigned to a specific gender, while those referring to *fire* or *dangerous* things (snakes, stinging nettles, and the like) are assigned to other gender categories. Lakoff noted that this type of "rule" was hardly arbitrary, but reflected specific cultural perceptions of the Dyirbal. So, Lakoff concluded, grammatical categories are hardly innate structures, as claimed by UG theory; rather, they are constructed to reflect differential perceptions of the world.

Today, linguistic anthropology and cognitive linguistics share many common interests, including the relation between linguistic categories, perception, and cultural worldviews, and how these manifest themselves in such systems as kinship organization, ethics, and the like. As a simple case in point, consider how the English language uses the single word *uncle* to refer to a mother's brother, a father's brother, and the husband of one's aunt. Other languages have a word for each of these relationships, suggesting differences in the roles played by "uncles" in different cultures. This simple example is multiplied throughout the lexicons of different languages.

Linguistic Relativity

The notion that language and thought are interconnected has ancient roots, as mentioned (Aarsleff 1982; Lucy 1985, 1997a; Seuren 1998). The Sophist philosopher Gorgias, for instance, maintained that reality cannot be experienced except through language, in contrast to Plato, who maintained that the world was the same for everyone and that a language simply labeled it differently (McComiskey 2002). The Greek historian Herodotus prefigured the LRH when he claimed, in his *Historia* (c. 430 BCE), that Egyptians thought differently than Greeks because they wrote from right to left, rather than from left to right, as did the Greeks. With this assertion, Herodotus seems to have understood two implicit principles that presaged linguistic anthropology: first, access to how the mind works is via cultural systems, such as writing; and, second, the mind is not a rigid entity—it is shaped by situational factors. A similar view was articulated by the fourteenth-century Algerian scholar Ibn Khaldun, who wrote a truly fascinating treatise in which he noted that the subtle mental and behavioral differences that existed between nomadic and city-dwelling Bedouins were due to differences in the vocabulary used by the two groups.

One of the first attempts to include this notion into a theory of language is the one by German philologist Friedrich Max Müller (1864: ii), who stated tersely that "language is identical with thought." As Sapir (1921) was to observe later, it became clear that a sense was crystallizing in the eighteenth and nineteenth centuries that the thought patterns exhibited by speakers of different languages are not the same ones with different verbal labels attached; rather, the labels themselves are windows into how the thought patterns are formed. Sapir also emphasized that this does not close thought down—a view that came to be known a little later as *linguistic determinism*—but, rather, that thought is simply *dependent* on patterns expressed in language. In 1976, Roger Brown referred to these two versions of the LRH as *strong* and *weak*, a distinction that has remained to this day.

TWO VERSIONS OF THE LRH

Strong: version which claims that language *determines* thought. This version is called *linguistic determinism*.

Weak: version which claims that language and its usage *influence* thought and behaviors, not determine them.

It is the weak version that is of specific interest in this book, although there is some question as to what it means, as will be discussed in due course.

A topic that began to rise to prominence in the eighteenth century in debates about language concerned the connection between language, ethnicity, and character. German philosopher and mathematician Gottfried Leibniz, for instance, envisioned a direct correlation between properties of the German language and what he saw as stereotypical traits of Germans themselves, including how they walked: "in the concatenation and inner sequence of our periods [sentences] we can observe the gait of a German, to whom a uniform, steady, and manly gait is peculiar" (Leibniz 1714: 44). As ludicrous as this might appear today, it nonetheless shows that the LRH was becoming a major theme in philosophy and philology. In 1746, the Swedish philosopher Emanuel Swedenborg observed that a language influenced how people viewed reality itself, leading to Johann Georg Hamann's concept of *Weltanschauung* ("worldview") (Betz 2009), an idea adopted a little later by Johann Gottfried von Herder (1772a, b: 99–100): "If it be true that we learn to think through words, then language is what defines and delineates the whole of human knowledge. In everyday life, it is clear that to think is almost nothing else but to speak. Every nation speaks according to the way it thinks and thinks according to the way it speaks." As philosopher Ernst Cassirer (1946: 12) wrote much later about Herder's view: "the distinctions which here are taken for granted, the analysis of reality in terms of things and processes, permanent and transitory aspects, objects and actions, do not precede language as a substratum of given fact, but that language itself is what initiates such articulations, and develops them in its own sphere." It is relevant to note that Sapir wrote his MA thesis on Herder's book, *Origin of Language,* in which Herder maintains that thought coincides with the origin of language.

This line of inquiry culminated in the work of Prussian philologist Wilhelm von Humboldt (1836). Working on languages as different historically and structurally as Basque and the ancient Kawi language of Java, Humboldt came to the conclusion that the categories of a language reflected how their speakers imagined the world and expressed their "inner life" (von Humboldt 1836: x):

> The character and structure of a language expresses the inner life and knowledge of its speakers, and that languages must differ from one another in the same way and to the same degree as those who use them. Sounds do not become words until a meaning has been put into them, and this meaning embodies the thought of a community.

Humboldt then went on to link a person's inner life with the *innere Sprachform* ("internal linguistic structure"), which generates the forms of a language itself and reflects what is in the minds of its speakers (von Humboldt 1836: 43):

> The central fact of language is that speakers can make infinite use of the finite resources provided by their language. Though the capacity for language is universal, the individuality of each language is a property of the people who speak it. Every language has its *innere Sprachform*, or internal structure, which determines its outer form and which is a reflection of its speakers' minds. The language and the thought of a people are thus inseparable.

Interestingly, Noam Chomsky, a staunch opponent of the LRH, espoused many of the ideas of Humboldt (Chomsky 1966, 1975), likely because the

German scholar considered human language to be a rule-governed system, rather than just a set of words and phrases paired with meanings. But there are profound differences between Humboldt and Chomsky. The former sees the rules as ontogenetic forms that guide the thoughts of a people; the latter sees the rules as part of an innate UG, not as shapers of thought. Humboldt's views are, actually, the direct forerunners of the twentieth-century formulations of LRH, based on his concept of *Weltansicht*, or linguistic worldview, as separate from *Weltanschauung*, or overall worldview (Wierzbicka 1996, 1997; Langham 2009; Underhill 2011, 2102).

Humboldt's views influenced the unstated research agenda of early linguistic anthropology, constituting principles that directly inspired Edward Sapir in the 1920s and later Benjamin Lee Whorf (Sapir's student at Yale University) in the 1930s. Whorf posited that languages predisposed their speakers to attend to certain concepts as being necessary. But, as he also emphasized, this does not mean that understanding between speakers of different languages is blocked. On the contrary, through translation and paraphrase people are always finding ways to understand each other. Moreover, the resources of any language allow its speakers to invent new categories any time they want, according to need, thus modifying worldviews. As Whorf (1956: 213) concisely and eloquently put it: "Language is not merely a reproducing instrument for voicing ideas but rather is itself the shaper of ideas." As American linguist and psychologist John Lucy (2001: 903) has astutely pointed out, linguistic relativity must be distinguished from "simple linguistic diversity and from strict linguistic determinism," given that these are often confused in the debates over the LRH. The LRH actually makes a claim that many would find uncontroversial—namely, that the specific language people speak *shapes* their thoughts, not determines them in any rigid way.

Perhaps the most important aspect of the LRH is that it identifies cultural thinking with cultural making—a principle that can be traced at least as far back as the *New Science*, written by the seventeen-eighteenth century philosopher Giambattista Vico (Bergin and Fisch 1984). For Vico, we create language not to just label the world, but to make sense of it, especially when it comes to abstractions that cannot be demonstrated in physical reality. Take the notion of "depth," for instance. In English, we talk about *profound* thoughts—a word that contains the Latin *fundus* "bottom." This is a metaphorical model of actual physical depth that has become an unconscious vehicle for conveying mental depth. Indeed, the latter can only be thought of in terms of its physical counterpart. Vico maintained that such modeling illustrates how we transfer sensory thinking to abstract thinking—a topic to be discussed subsequently. As Arnheim (1969: 233) has aptly observed: "Human thinking cannot go beyond the patterns suppliable by the human senses."

Investigating Linguistic Relativity

As intriguing as it is, is there any psychological substance to the LRH? Can it even be investigated empirically? As discussed at the start of this chapter, a common method of investigating the LRH by linguists is via comparisons between languages. Another is by examining translation anomalies that arise between languages. Added to these two main linguistic methods, psychology has devised various experiments to test its validity (as we shall see). Within all such approaches, the notion of *relativity effects* has been adopted either overtly or implicitly. This refers to the effects that shape perception and thinking at the specific levels of language.

RELATIVITY EFFECTS AT THE DIFFERENT LANGUAGE LEVELS

Phonology: the level of vocal sounds. Linguists distinguish between *phonetic* and *phonemic* components of phonology. The former is the inventory of sounds (consonants, vowels, etc.) that a language possesses, and the latter is the organization of the sounds into units, called *phonemes*, that signal differences in the meaning of words. The relativity effects at this level may involve how phonemes shape the perception of certain referents.

Morphology: (as discussed above) the level on which words are constructed with morphemes. The relativity effects here may vary according to the type of language (agglutinative, isolating, etc.) or according to how specific morphemes (such as verb suffixes) may index specific cultural categories (such as time).

Syntax: (also as mentioned) the level on which morphemes and lexemes are combined to form larger structures. The relativity effects at this level concern how these structures may influence how speakers view the interconnection of events in the world.

Semantics: the level at which the different morphemes and lexemes cohere into meaning-bearing structures. The relativity effects at this level may involve how words, for example, filter information and shape its interpretation.

Pragmatics: the use of language for various social purposes, such as daily communication, writing, and so on. The relativity effects at this level may manifest themselves in shaping communicative functions such as greeting and politeness protocols.

Overall, the findings from the different research methods have shown that the language–thought nexus is not rigid, neither is it impervious to change. However, as we shall see throughout this text, they also suggest that the linguistic categories acquired in childhood shape how thoughts are formed and then delivered subsequently. In English, for example, verbs must specify tense; as a consequence, speakers must attend to the time frame when an event occurred. In Turkish, on the other hand, verbs indicate whether past events were witnessed or not; as a result, speakers attend to corroboration of the events, not just their indication. The study of verb systems has in effect indicated that speakers of different languages understand time-based events differentially (Slobin Dan 1996; Wolff and Holmes 2011).

Despite such supporting findings on relativity effects, fundamental questions remain: Is linguistic relativity real in any neurocognitive sense? What happens in the brain before and after language? There is some neuroscientific evidence that language does indeed guide cognition, but it is not strong—to be discussed subsequently. Another question that is difficult to address in any empirical way is: How does language change adaptively to reflect new realities and how is it tied to creativity in a species-specific way? (Deacon 1997; Maturana and Varela 1973).

Despite such lingering questions, the LRH has nonetheless had many implications for the study of language and its connection to thought, culture, and society. Like Korzybski's anecdote, it illustrates how language and mind interact in specific ways across cultural systems. Consider writing style differences. Speakers of English, who are accustomed to writing from left to write, tend to imagine *past* time as a "left-oriented" phenomenon and *future* time as a "right oriented" one. To grasp what this means, consider a straight line segment, which has a point on it labeled *Now* located in the center of the line. Where would a speaker of English put the verbal labels *Before* and *After* on that line? A speaker would almost certainly put *Before* to the left and *After* to the right of *Now*. Why so? A plausible explanation is that English writing goes from the left side of a page to the right. So, something that has been written "before" is left-based in the visual space and something that is written "after" is right-based in that same visual space. Those who are accustomed to writing and reading from right to left will tend to reverse the order of the labels, for the same reason. The allocation of the three words on the line also reflects English verb tenses marked for *present*, *past*, and *future*. These, too, are perceived to lie on a mental *timeline*, with *past* placed before (to the left of) the *present*, and *future* placed after (to the right). However, this kind of explanation raises a chicken-and-egg question: Which came first, the language or the linear conceptualization? All that can be said is that the two, language and conceptualization, are intertwined inextricably.

Consider another example. English speakers say that they read something *in a newspaper*. The use of the preposition *in* implies that the newspaper is imagined as a container of information *into which* one must go to seek it out. That is why speakers also say that they *got a lot out of the newspaper*, or that there *was nothing in it*. On the other hand, Italian speakers use the preposition *su* ("on"), implying that the information is perceived as being impressed on the surface of the pages. Therefore, there are no expressions similar to *we got a lot out of the newspaper* and *there was nothing in it*. This particular kind of relativity effect occurs in the domain of metaphorical language—to be discussed subsequently.

Critiques

The most effective critiques against the LRH have actually been those aimed at linguistic determinism, rather than linguistic relativity in itself, which has been much harder to reject. As Whorf (Whorf 1956: 213–214) observed, linguistic relativity implies the following: "We cut nature up, organize it into concepts, and ascribe significances as we do, largely because we are parties to an agreement to organize it in this way—an agreement that holds throughout our speech community and is codified in the patterns of our language." As Sapir and Swadesh (1946: 106) cogently pointed out, this does not mean that a language blocks understanding among speakers of different languages:

> It would be naïve to imagine that any analysis of experience is dependent on pattern expressed in language. Any concept, whether or not it forms part of the system of grammatical categories, can be conveyed in any language. If a notion is lacking in a given series, it implies a different configuration and not a lack of expressive power.

The most biting critiques of linguistic relativity came after Chomsky put forth his universalist theory of language in the late 1950s and early 1960s (1957, 1965). By the 1970s, the LRH even became an object of ridicule among a number of linguists (Schaff 1973). The strongest evidence that seemed to support the Chomskyan-based critiques came from anthropologists Brent Berlin and Paul Kay in their study of color terminology in 1969—to which we will return. Suffice it to say here that it seemed to show the presence of universal patterns in color naming. So, what had previously been claimed to constitute a supporting case in point for the LRH, turned out seemingly to be a counterargument against it.

German-American linguist Ekkehart Malotki (1983) attacked many of the points made by Whorf about the Hopi verb tense system, challenging Whorf's central tenet that the Hopi verb system is connected to a worldview that is "timeless." But Whorf did not claim categorically that the Hopi language did not mark time—rather, he maintained that it did so differently (Whorf 1940: 236): "It [the Hopi language] recognizes psychological time, which is much like Bergson's 'duration,' but this 'time' is quite unlike the mathematical time, T, used by our physicists." By using the term "timeless," Whorf was contrasting the different views of space and time that exist between Hopi and Standard Average European (SAE) languages (see Chapter 3).

> **HOPI SOCIETY**
>
> The Hopi are a Native American society who live primarily in north-eastern Arizona as a sovereign nation within the USA. There are fewer than 20,000 Hopi today. The Hopi language is one of several dozen Uto-Aztecan languages and is, unfortunately, on the verge of disappearing. Because, in the sixteenth century, the Hopi encountered Spaniards who intermingled with them, some of their villages have Spanish names, and they are sometimes called the Pueblo people (after *pueblos*—"villages," in Spanish).
>
> The name *Hopi* is an abbreviated form of the expression "the peaceful people," which encapsulates the Hopi's worldview—a total reverence and respect for all things. They observe their traditional ceremonies for the benefit of the entire world. Whorf became fascinated by Hopi culture and how the language of the Hopi encoded their peaceful worldview.

Whorf claimed that there was no lexeme in Hopi that corresponded to the English noun *time*. Nonetheless, it has concrete ways of referring to temporal events; for example, *pàasa* ("for that long"), *pàasat* ("at that time"), *hisat* ("occasion to do something"), *aw nánaptsiwta* ("to have time for something"). Whorf argued that, unlike SAE languages, Hopi had "no general notion or intuition of time as a smooth flowing continuum in which everything in the universe proceeds at equal rate, out of a future, through the present, into a past" (Whorf 1956: 57). One of Malotki's more effective counterarguments consisted in providing examples of Hopi linguistic units referring to temporal relations that appeared to show, contrary to Whorf's assertion, a progression from past, through the present, into the future. However, this did not put an end to the debate on time, as will be discussed in Chapter 3 (see Leavitt 2011; Lee 1991, 1996).

The anti-Whorfian stream in linguistics became widespread after Malotki's study. Steven Pinker (1994) rejected the LRH outright as specious speculation, maintaining that thought is independent of language, originating in what he called "mentalese," a frame of mind that precedes speech. Whatever "mentalese" means, it is clear that it, too, is unprovable, ironically, in the same way as the LRH. Where is this mentalese in the brain? How does it lead to language? Other linguists have actually referred to the LRH as a "great language hoax" (Martin 1986; McWhorter 2016;

Pullum 1991), using Whorf's own analysis of Inuit terms for "snow" against him (Whorf 1940: 238):

> We have the same word for falling snow, snow on the ground, snow packed hard like ice, slushy snow, wind-driven flying snow—whatever the situation may be. To an [Inuit], this all-inclusive word would be almost unthinkable; he would say that falling snow, slushy snow, and so on, are sensuously and operationally different, different things to contend with; he uses different words for them and for other kinds of snow. The Aztecs go even farther than we in the opposite direction, with "cold," "ice," and "snow" all represented by the same basic word with different terminations; "ice" is the noun form; "cold," the adjectival form; and for "snow," "ice mist."

Laura Martin (1986) argued that Whorf's analysis was an utter misinterpretation. Where Inuit has individual lexemes, English uses phrases and expressions to refer to the same stretches of reality. Geoffrey Pullum (1991) concurred—morphemes such as *qani-* for "snowflake" and *apu-* for "snow lying on the ground or covering things up"—are equivalents of English *slush*. So, the perceptual mechanisms are the same, only the linguistic ones differ, and they do not affect those mechanisms—a critique made as well by McWhorter (2016). But, overall, these critiques are themselves anecdotal and thus do not impugn Whorf's basic argument that snow is a unitary concept in English, but not so in Inuit, which has developed a specialized vocabulary for it necessitated by the vital role that it plays (or has historically played) in Inuit life.

What this implies, in effect, is that Inuit and English speakers have different "pictures in their minds," to recall how Whorf phrased it (see above). Recall also that Whorf made an analogy between linguistic relativity and relativity in physics to explain such differential views of the world, claiming that science and linguistics have a lot in common, as he observes (Whorf 1940: 234–235):

> The situation here is not unlike that in any other field of science. All real scientists have their eyes primarily on background phenomena that cut very little ice, as such, in our daily lives; yet their studies have a way of bringing out a close relation between these unsuspected realms of fact and such decidedly foreground activities as transporting goods, preparing food, treating the sick, or growing potatoes, which in time may become very much modified, simply because of pure scientific investigation in no way concerned with these brute matters themselves. Linguistics presents a quite similar case; the background phenomena with which it deals are involved in all our

> foreground activities of talking and of reaching agreement, in all reasoning and arguing of cases, in all law, arbitration, conciliation, contracts, treaties, public opinion, weighing of scientific theories, formulation of scientific results. Whenever agreement or assent is arrived at in human affairs, and whether or not mathematics or other specialized symbolisms are made part of the procedure, this agreement is reached by linguistic processes, or else it is not reached.

As Penny Lee (1996) has cogently argued, the theory of relativity in physics actually played an influential role in shaping Whorf's notion of linguistic relativity. For example, he noted that Hopi verbs refer to events in space and time that are marked simultaneously as objective and subjective. Whorf explained this peculiar feature of the Hopi language as inceptive—a feature which indicates that something that exists in space and time will mean something slightly different to a speaker who uses it in a context. Overall, the Hopi verb system coincides with the quantum view of *spacetime* as a unitary concept, where *space* and *time* are no longer viewed as separate entities, as Albert Einstein famously said in 1906 (cited in Robins: 70):

> The views of space and time which I wish to lay before you have sprung from the soil of experimental physics, and therein lies their strength. They are radical. Henceforth, space by itself, and time by itself, are doomed to fade away into mere shadows, and only a kind of union of the two will preserve an independent reality.

Epilogue

Whorf never conceived of relativity effects as being weak or strong, as they came to be labeled by Brown (1976) much later; he envisioned what can be called a "relativity continuum" on which the effects can be stronger or weaker; that is, there are some effects produced by a particular language that strongly shape perception according to specific levels and categories, others less so. This comes out especially in translation, where linguistic gaps between two languages create problems of thought to greater or lesser degrees, not in the absolute. These are remedied by paraphrases and extrapolations, but the thought patterns of the two languages, encoded by differential linguistic structures, never really coincide on the continuum.

As mentioned, the word *hypothesis* was added later to Whorf's concept of linguistic relativity, to indicate that it was supposition or putative explanation requiring further investigation. It was Harry Hoijer (1954), another of Sapir's students, who introduced the term the "Sapir–Whorf *hypothesis*," in homage to both scholars. For the most part, work on the

LRH has focused on level analysis (morphological, syntactic, lexical, and so on), as pointed out above. But after Hymes' introduction of the concept of communicative competence, the research paradigm has been extended to include pragmatic aspects.

Alfred Korzybski, whose anecdote was used at the start of this chapter, made a statement that has now become a famous one that encapsulates the LRH: "The map is not the territory it represents, but, if correct, it has a similar structure to the territory, which accounts for its usefulness" (Korzybski 1933: 58). Now, as will be discussed subsequently, language is actually one map of the world that humans have devised; there are other kinds of maps, which produce the same kinds of relativity effects.

As a case in point, consider the type of figures that produce optical illusions, such as those that impel us to perceive different figures at different times in the same picture, as in the famous *duck–rabbit illusion*, noted by psychologist Joseph Jastrow in 1899. As we look at the picture, either a duck or a rabbit comes into focus at different instances of viewing (Figure 1.1).

The illusion is caused because of similarities in the picture that our brain interprets ambiguously; these make it impossible to control the shift. The same applies to words. A word such as *lion* is interpreted both denotatively (as a particular kind of animal) and connotatively (as a human character trait)—and the shift in this case is guided by the context of use. This same pattern, incidentally, has been found with the above illusion. Children shown the illusion on Easter Sunday are more likely to see the figure as a rabbit, whereas when shown the same image on a Sunday in October, they tend to see it as a duck (Brugger and Brugger 1993). This is indirect evidence that we are influenced by labels and how they are situated in specific ways—a topic that has been investigated in an in-depth way by researchers of the LRH, as will be discussed. For now, it is sufficient to point out that relativity effects occur in language and other semiotic systems. Studying why and how they occur is the overarching aim of the LRH.

FIGURE 1.1 The duck–rabbit illusion

Discussion Questions and Activities

Chapter Questions

After reading this chapter, how would you answer the questions on which it is based?

1. What is the notion of linguistic relativity?
2. What are its origins?
3. Is it relevant or useful to understanding the role of language in human life?

Related Questions

4. What are the main differences between views of language such as those expressed by "universalist" theorists such as the Port-Royale grammarians and Noam Chomsky and "relativists" such as Humboldt, Boas, Sapir, and Whorf? What arguments can be made for or against each one?
5. What do you think Whorf may have meant with the word *timeless* in characterizing the Hopi language?
6. Do you agree with the critiques leveled at Whorf's assessment of the different terms used for *snow* in Inuit?
7. The following excerpt is from Whorf (1940: 256). Do you agree with its main suggestions?

    Every normal person in the world, past infancy in years, can and does talk. By virtue of that fact, every person—civilized or uncivilized—carries through life certain naive but deeply rooted ideas about talking and its relation to thinking. Because of their firm connection with speech habits that have become unconscious and automatic, these notions tend to be rather intolerant of opposition. They are by no means entirely personal and haphazard; their basis is definitely systematic.

8. The main counterargument to the LRH is that each language encodes the same reality with different forms. Do you agree?

Activities

1. All languages have resources for making new words to encode new meanings. For example, English lacks a word for "the friend of a friend." If we decide to coin one, we would be guided by two main criteria: (1) it is likely best constructed as a noun; and (2) it must have the same type of structure as any English noun. So, words such as *defriend*

or *grandfriend*, would satisfy both criteria. Below are referents that are not encoded by English vocabulary. Make up single words for them.
   (a) a repeated mistake
   (b) the enemy of an enemy
   (c) walking slowly and lazily
   (d) acting quickly and energetically.
2. An assumption of Universal Grammar theory is that there exists a set of rule-making principles in the brain that undergird the construction of the grammars of different languages. If so, indicate whether you would see (or not see) the following as universal principles:
   (a) Basic sentences are formed from an underlying subject–verb–object (SVO) structure.
   (b) All sentences must have a verb.
   (c) The meaning of a sentence is determined by the organization of the structures in it.
3. Translation is often used as a method for researching relativity effects. Can you give examples of words in languages that cannot be translated into English? One example would be the French word *naïve*, which is not a native word in English.
4. Children are creative when it comes to filling in linguistic gaps they might have. Can you explain the following two (hypothetical) gap-fillers?
   (a) My father has a hole in his head (baldness).
   (b) There is a ball in the sky (moon).
5. If you know a language other than English, how would these terms be translated? Are there any differences in the concepts they enfold?
   (a) table
   (b) sadness
   (c) happiness.

2
EARLY RESEARCH ON LINGUISTIC RELATIVITY

Prologue

One of Lewis Carroll's most interesting pieces of writing is his poem about a strange dragon-like monster called the Jabberwock, which he included in his children's novel *Through the Looking-Glass, and What Alice Found There* (1871). Titled "Jabberwocky", many of the words in the poem are nonsensical, even though they have the feel of English word structure. Like Alice in the story, we somehow feel impelled to figure out what they could possibly (or potentially) mean. The first four lines are:

>Twas brillig, and the slithy toves
>Did gyre and gimble in the wabe;
>All mimsy were the borogoves,
>And the mome raths outgrabe.

Because they are constructed morphologically as are actual English words, they prompt us to attach suggestive meanings to them. Some of these are provided by Carroll himself. For instance, he explained the word "Jabberwock" as a blend of the Anglo-Saxon word *wocor* (meaning "offspring") with *jabber* (in its ordinary meaning of "excited and voluble discussion") (Tenniel 2003: 328–331). In another part of the novel, Humpty Dumpty comments that *brillig* "means four o'clock in the afternoon, the time when you begin broiling things for dinner." Alice defines *wabe* as "the grass-plot around a sundial," to which Humpty Dumpty retorts, "Of course, it is," because it "goes a long way before it, and a long way behind it." In effect, Jabberwocky shows that forms constructed artificially to resemble actual words will impel us to assign meanings to them on the basis of similarities and analogies to existing things. If Jabberwocky words were to become part of the English lexicon, then they would make the meanings they evoke systematic and habitual—that is, speakers would start "seeing" or "recognizing" *brilligs, slithy toves,* and *wabes* everywhere. Carroll was clearly fascinated by the connection between language and mind. His writings dovetailed with the advent of linguistic science in the nineteenth century, prefiguring the notion of linguistic relativity, which was adopted shortly after his death as a principle of language by linguists in the first decades of the twentieth century—an era that can thus be called the first era of linguistic relativity study.

This chapter looks at that era, starting with the ideas of Franz Boas, who saw the study of different languages as a means to understanding how they served the specific cognitive-cultural needs of its speakers, and then those of Boas' student at Columbia University, Edward Sapir. Sapir explicitly asserted that people's perception of reality is shaped by the language they speak: "The fact of the matter is that the 'real world' is to a large extent unconsciously built upon the language habits of the group. No two languages are ever sufficiently similar to be considered as representing the same social reality" (Sapir 1929: 207). The ideas of Russian psychologist Lev Vygotsky will also be discussed as they pertain to the LRH.

The questions that will guide the discussion in this chapter are:

1. What does it mean to assert that a specific language is tied to the particular experiences of a culture?
2. Does language and thought form a continuum?
3. How was the language-thought-culture nexus researched initially?

Franz Boas and Edward Sapir

Franz Boas' research at Columbia University in the first decade of the twentieth century laid the groundwork for investigating linguistic relativity in a meaningful way. Even though he never explicitly used that term, it was implied in his analysis of the research he conducted on indigenous cultures of North America, from which he came to the general conclusion that a language emerges historically to reflect the environmental and social experiences of their speakers, serving their specific intellectual and communicative needs. This can be seen in the overall grammar and lexicon that a language develops over time, but it can also be seen even in individual structures within them. For instance, the English language has very few words for *seals*, whereas the languages of those who live in the Arctic have a sophisticated specialized vocabulary to refer to them. As seemingly trivial as this observation may seem, in a Boasian framework it is a concrete piece of data on how different cultures organize their social worlds differentially through words. This became a principle for conducting research in early linguistic anthropology.

Boas adopted the method of ethnography (originally called ethnology) to carry out his research, whereby researchers would live among the peoples they studied and wrote about (Lowie 1917; Boas 1920; Malinowski 1922). Information-gathering was thus based on participant observation—that is, by living among the informants and experiencing their way of life. It was the Russian-German historian and geographer, Gerhard Friedrich Müller, who had introduced this method in the eighteenth century (Vermeulen 2015). But it was Boas (1920) who installed it as the major research paradigm of linguistic anthropology, distinguishing between *ethnology* as the study of the characteristics of different people and *ethnography* as the description of those characteristics. In practice, today only the latter term is used in linguistic anthropology.

Boas' underlying premise was that a particular language evolved adaptively to allow its speakers to refer to, and interpret, those things, ideas, and values that are of significance to their everyday life. The lexicon of a language is thus much more than an arbitrary repertory of verbal labels about the things of the world; it is a means with which to interpret them meaningfully in social terms. In English, we use descriptive terms (usually adjectives, metaphors, and the like) for referring to seals: for example, *bull seal* and *elephant seal*, which are analogies to other animals that the seals appear to resemble. But, in various Inuit indigenous languages, the lexicon is much more specialized culturally in this domain of reference. For instance, these languages have a general term for "seal," another one for "seal basking in the sun," a third one for a "seal floating on a piece of ice," and so on. The reason is that, in a Boasian framework, seals play a significant role in these cultures and this is reflected in the Inuit lexicon.

Boas (1911/1963: 149) provided what is now considered to be the first anthropological definition of *culture*:

> The totality of the mental and physical reactions and activities that characterize the behavior of the individuals composing a social group collectively and individually in relation to their natural environment, to other groups, to members of the group itself, and of each individual to himself.

To gain access to a people's "mental and physical reactions and activities," the anthropologist must learn their language—hence the need for participant observation and ethnography. Boas was also among the first to attack deterministic views of languages, stressing the equal worth of all cultures and languages, and that there was no such thing as a "better" or "worse" language or culture. As he put it: "No one has ever proved that a human being, through his descent from a certain group of people, must of necessity have certain mental characteristics" (Boas 1945: 23). To avoid falling into the trap of judging others during fieldwork, Boas required his student ethnographers to learn the native language of the culture that they studied and to appreciate what it told them about those among whom they would live. His overall perspective was that, even though diversity is a principle of life, there is still a commonality of understanding that links humans together as one race.

Boas focused mainly on vocabulary as providing access points into a culture's worldview. It was Sapir (1921) who extended Boas' approach to encompass grammar, including the syntactic structure of sentences. For an example of what this may imply, consider the different layout of the same three words in English:

1. *Chris teased Daniela*; and
2. *Daniela teased Chris*.

Reversing the subject and the predicate is not a simple permutation of the words; in so doing, the meaning of the sentences is also reversed. The reason is that the arrangement of words in English sentences mirrors an actor-action-receiver relationship. The actor is converted into the grammatical subject of an active English sentence, the action into a verb, and the receiver into its aim (or object). In example (1) *Chris* is the actor, whereas in example (2) it is *Daniela*. In example (1) *Daniela* is the receiver of the teasing action, whereas in example (2) the receiver is *Chris*. This change in order is why the meanings are also reversed. In effect, syntax (word order) in English determines meaning. Sapir (1921) argued that by analyzing such differences, we would gain an understanding of how a grammatical structure, such as the sentence, shapes unconscious psychological forces at work in interpreting the world. As he put it (Sapir 1921: 87): "The sentence is the outgrowth of historical and of unreasoning psychological forces rather than of a logical synthesis of elements that have been clearly grasped in their individuality." Sapir went on to suggest that syntax is not an arbitrary system of rules of sentence formation; it is a guide to how thoughts are formed and shaped, as the above example shows. By becoming accustomed to using a certain type of grammar (agglutinative, isolating, and so on), there is a doubling-back effect on the mind, that is, the linguistic categories in the grammar shape how we understand reality. To cite Sapir (1921: 75):

> Human beings do not live in the object world alone, nor alone in the world of social activity as ordinarily understood, but are very much at the mercy of the particular language system which has become the

medium of expression for their society. It is quite an illusion to imagine that one adjusts to reality essentially without the use of language and that language is merely an incidental means of solving specific problems of communication or reflection. The fact of the matter is that the "real world" is to a large extent unconsciously built up on the language habits of the group.

What we see and hear is thus guided by the language habits in our minds, which predispose us to make certain interpretations of reality as it presents itself to us. So, "the worlds in which different societies live are distinct worlds, not merely the same worlds with different labels attached" (Sapir 1921: 76). Sapir also maintained that a particular grammar affected how things are recalled. As speculative as this may seem, the number of studies that have subsequently given substance to his assertion is actually very large. Consider as a case in point a study by John Lucy (1996) that looked at the effects of grammatical differences on memory tasks in English and Yucatec (a Mayan language). English requires a plural morpheme (such as /-s/) for its count nouns, whether or not they refer to animate beings or inanimate objects (*cat-cats, table-tables*); but it does not mark the plural of mass nouns (*rice, corn*, etc.). Yucatec, on the other hand, does not have plural markers in the same way, treating its nouns morphologically like mass nouns. When Lucy presented pictures of Yucatec village scenes, English speakers were able to recall not only the number of animate beings but also the number of objects in the scenes; Yucatec speakers showed difficulties in this respect; they recalled other aspects of the scenes holistically. Although this is a highly reductive paraphrase of this insightful experiment, the point is that it brings out how the particular categories of a language may influence recall.

Sapir set the stage for conducting specific kinds of research on relativity effects on the various levels of languages, from the lexical to the pragmatic, thus expanding the Boasian paradigm cross-linguistically.

CROSS-LINGUISTIC RESEARCH

Lexical: This level lends itself concretely to testing relativity effects via cross-linguistic comparison. In English, for example, the anatomical part starting at the shoulder and ending at the fingertips is lexicalized as *arm* and *hand*. Refinements to this lexical dichotomy exist (*upper arm, wrist*), of course, but they are connected semantically (and conceptually) to either the hand or the arm. In Russian, no such distinction has been coded lexically. The word *ruká* refers to the whole appendage (*arm + hand* in English). Russians can refer to the difference between arms and hands in other ways, if the situation requires them to do so.

> *Grammatical:* On this level, as we saw above, relativity effects can be studied in terms of such patterns as word order and plural marking, which may indicate differences in various cognitive processes such as memory.
>
> *Semantic:* This level involves the cross-linguistic study of the relativity effects connected to the meanings of words and other semantic structures. For instance, the word *simpatico* in Italian cannot be rendered directly in English as a single lexeme; rather, its semantic range must be rendered with paraphrases, approximations, and so on (*likeable, easy to get along with, pleasant*, etc.).
>
> *Pragmatic:* The ways in which speech acts are structured in everyday conversations, such as how the speakers of different languages greet each other or convey social respect, constitutes an area of investigation on relativity effects that took hold after Hymes' (1971) introduction of the notion of communicative competence (to be discussed in Chapter 5).

Sapir had retrieved, in effect, the Humboldtian idea that language structure (*innere Sprachform*) and worldview are intertwined. This comes out anecdotally each time we attempt to translate words from one language to another—the translation is rarely exact; it is mainly approximate. On the other hand, Sapir explicitly rejected linguistic determinism by stating: "It would be naïve to imagine that any analysis of experience is dependent on pattern expressed in language" (Sapir 1921: 23).

The early research on linguistic relativity raised several questions that remain unanswered to this day, which can be paraphrased as follows: What would a wordless thought be like? What would a thoughtless word be like? As we saw with "Jabberwocky," it is almost impossible to separate language and thought. When nonsense words are created, our instinctive response is to find meanings for them—that is, to come up with thoughts that are suggested by the linguistic forms themselves.

The premise of linguistic relativity that guided early research in linguistic anthropology came under criticism a little later, in 1953, by Eric Lenneberg, who held that the different meanings encoded by languages may not be coincident, but they are equivalent. Together with Roger Brown (Brown and Lenneberg 1954), Lenneberg then carried out a series of experiments directly testing the psychological validity of this premise, focusing on how speakers of different languages perceived color hues. In one experiment, speakers of English and Zuñi (a Pueblo society) were asked to name specific color stimuli, so as to determine whether their native color lexicon would influence their ability to name different hues. The researchers found that the length of the color name, the rapidity in naming, and the agreement in naming between the two languages were good indices of what they termed *codability*, defined as the degree to which speakers agree on a name for something. Brown and Lenneberg discovered that colors with the highest degree of codability occupied central positions on the color spectrum named in English as *red, orange, yellow, green, blue, purple, pink,* and *brown,* while colors with the lowest codability fell within transitional areas between any two such positions on the spectrum. They also found other interesting differences. For example, Zuñi speakers used one term that covered the same hue range of English *green* and *blue,* suggesting a different codability in this domain and thus that it may vary somewhat cross-linguistically. Overall, the findings suggested, as Brown commented in a later work (1958: 241), that "the more codable categories of experience are also more available and more codable stimuli are centrally located in available categories." So, rather than relativity effects in color perception, lexical differences in color reference can be explained in terms of codability. What may be a single-word name in one language may be rendered by a two-word distinction in another but, in terms of codability, they are close enough. We shall return to the debate on color terms in Chapter 4.

Later, Brown (1976: 128), who did not reject linguistic relativity outright, referred to it as having two versions—weak and strong, as discussed in Chapter 1. The weak version implies that "Structural differences between language systems will, in general, be paralleled by nonlinguistic cognitive differences, of an unspecified sort, in the native speakers of the language;" and the strong version that "The structure of anyone's native language strongly influences or fully determines the worldview he will acquire as he learns the language."

Lev S. Vygotsky

Russian psychologist Lev Vygotsky read Sapir's book *Language* (Sapir 1921), and was apparently inspired by it to study experimentally the ways in which the development of concepts in children was influenced by the language to which they were exposed. His 1934 work *Myshlenie i rech*, a collection of scholarly papers, translated in 1962 as *Thought and Language*, is now considered to be complementary to Sapir's book, providing supportive evidence of the influence of language on cognition. Vygotsky's experiments on language development establish connections between language acquisition and the development of mental concepts in childhood. As children acquire their particular language, their thoughts become more and more linked to its words, leading to a period that he designated as the *inner speech* phase, when children appear to be talking to themselves and thus thinking out loud, as they are apparently testing the relation between words and thoughts. The silent linguistic testing of thoughts actually remains as a pattern throughout life.

Vygotsky's work showed, overall, that children acquire language by guessing and experimenting with words, making analogies and inferences about the world that recall Carroll's "Jabberwocky" mind game. Before two years of age, speech and thought develop in differing ways along with differing functions. By the age of two, however, thought becomes indistinguishable from the semantic structures in the language being acquired and what they allow children to do socially. For example, the instant children discover that the word *no* allows them to express displeasure and to achieve a reaction from interlocutors, they start using it repetitively, testing out its socio-regulatory possibilities.

Vygotsky documented developmental stages that go from external (physical and social) actions toward internal cognitive constructions and inner speech. The earliest words are hardly simple descriptions of the world, rather they are images akin to fables: "The primary word is not a straightforward symbol for a concept but rather an image, a picture, a mental sketch of a short concept, a short tale about it—indeed, a small work of art" (Vygotsky 1972: 298). In one experiment (Vygotsky 1931), he showed how a color that is verbalized with a specific word becomes what that language says it is, thus prefiguring the relativistic work on color terms. In another set of experiments, he demonstrated that sentences are not processed as a combination of the thoughts associated with the individual constituent words but, rather, with a holistic assessment of the meaning of the combination itself: "thought does not consist of individual words, [it] is always something whole, something with significantly greater extent and volume than the individual word" (Vygotsky 1984: 289–290).

Vygotsky's ideas stand in contrast with subsequent innatist views of language acquisition, such as Universal Grammar (UG) theory (Chapter 1) and the Poverty of the Stimulus notion, both formulated by Chomsky (1980, 1986). The latter was Chomsky's reformulation of Plato's problem: How is it that children, whose contacts with the world are brief and limited, are able to use and understand language spontaneously? Chomsky concluded that the only plausible answer to this question was that language was an innate faculty and that a specific language is drafted from this faculty (called the UG) based on the specific speech input to which the child is exposed.

UNIVERSAL GRAMMAR

Universal Grammar (UG), formulated by Noam Chomsky, claims that languages are built on the basis of the same set of rule-making principles that guide children to construct the specific grammars of the languages they acquire in context—when the child learns one rule about a specific language,

> the child can easily infer other rules without having to learn them one by one, mapping them from the UG onto the input. These rules are part of a neural mechanism for combining verbal symbols in specific ways—a process that Chomsky calls *merge*. It is this process that causes language to be what it is.
>
> This notion derives indirectly from Richard Montague's (1974) argument that languages are based on rules of logic, such as the rule of compositionality, which asserts that the meaning of the whole is a function of the meanings of its parts via rules of combination. In this framework, idiomatic expressions such as *wild goose chase* or *tip of the iceberg* are seen as unitary lexical items—that is, as singular lexemes that are composed of separate parts that cannot be isolated as in literal speech, thus marginalizing the role of figurative language in verbal development (Chapter 6).

It is not surprising to find that many of those who dismiss the notion of linguistic relativity are also supportive of the Chomskyan paradigm. Pullum and Scholz (2002), for example, provided arguments for the Poverty of the Stimulus notion, which explains why children, despite not receiving explicit instructions, come to understand spontaneously what is possible or not possible in a language, and why they do so despite the "deficient" quality of the linguistic input to which they are exposed, which is replete with errors, false starts, and so on. Furthermore, since other organisms in the same environment do not acquire language, the implication is that only humans are hard-wired to do so. Without going into details here, there are many counterarguments to this perspective (for example, Cowie 1999). For instance, the emergence of grammar in children can be explained instead as a process of creative extrapolation from the patterns present in the linguistic input to which they are exposed. This is why they constantly create analogies to existing concepts via the limited vocabulary they have acquired. If they learn that *ball* stands for something with a spherical shape, then they apply this word analogously to anything with this shape, such as the *moon*. Moreover, a feature of input-processing is the discarding (not merging) of information. One of the main tasks of the brain is, in fact, to filter information that is either irrelevant, or else unrelated to need. Language is such a filtering device.

Vygotsky (1962) saw creative aspects of language, such as metaphor, as vital clues to understanding how it is acquired. As mentioned, children make inferences and analogies about the things in the world that are evident in their first words. When they do not know how to label something—such as *baldness*—they resort to analogies or metaphor, calling it perhaps *a hole in the head*. Such "poetic fables," as Vygotsky called them, allow children to fill in conceptual gaps. Gradually, these are replaced by the words they acquire in context, which then refine (filter) their thoughts from then on. By the time of puberty children have become creatures of their language, which has become a template for the filtering and organization of information.

Throughout his work Vygotsky was adamant about emphasizing that language and thought form a unified whole—one cannot exist without the other. He considered that (1962: 223):

> A word without meaning is an empty sound: meaning, therefore, is a criterion of "word," its indispensable component. But from the point of view of psychology, the meaning of every word is a generalization or a concept. And since generalizations and concepts are undeniably acts of thought, we may regard meaning as a phenomenon of thinking. It does not follow, however, that meaning formally belongs in two different spheres of psychic life. Word meaning is a phenomenon of thought only in so far as speech is connected with thought and illuminated by it. It is a phenomenon of verbal thought, or meaningful speech—a union of word and thought.

Along with the work of Boas and Sapir, Vygotsky's research emerged to shed significant light on linguistic relativity from a developmental perspective. It showed that thought can occur separately from language, as it does in preverbal children. But after language is acquired, the two become intertwined and when gaps between language and thought occur, they are filled creatively with poetic fables; namely, with figurative concepts that, as we shall see (Chapter 6), are crucial in completing the overall theory of linguistic relativity.

Relevant Research Questions

An ingenious psychological experiment was conducted by Carmichael, Hogan, and Walter in 1932 to test the validity of relativity effects in a specific way. The researchers found that when they showed subjects a picture and then asked them later to reproduce it as a drawing, their recall was influenced by the verbal label assigned to the picture. For instance, one picture they showed consisted of two circles joined by a straight line. To one group of subjects (group A), the label *eyeglasses* was provided for the picture; to another (group B) the label used was *dumbbells*. When asked to draw what they saw a little later, group A reproduced the figure typically as an object resembling "eyeglasses;" while group B reproduced it as something resembling "dumbbells." Clearly, the label given to the picture influenced its recall. The same picture with no verbal cues was shown to a control group, which did not reproduce drawings that were influenced in a similar way.

32 Early Research on Linguistic Relativity

Follow-up studies showed some divergence from this intriguing finding. Prentice (1954), for instance, tested the effects of verbal labels on recognition instead of recall, finding that the labels did not affect recognition. However, recognition is different from recall in some ways. So, the results of the Carmichael-Hogan-Walter study have never been refuted outright. It showed that relativity effects manifest themselves in concrete ways, such as connecting words to a specific cognitive process—recall.

Starting at the end of the nineteenth century, the study of perception in terms of visual perception was producing findings that have retroactively become relevant to the understanding of relativity effects (Bates 1923; (Bühler 1907; Parsons 1927; Wundt 1898)). Consider the lines in Figure 2.1: Which appears to be the longer line?

People raised in Western cultures typically see the middle line as longer than the other two, even though the lines are equal in length. The likely source of the illusion, called the Müller-Lyer Illusion, after the German sociologist Franz Carl Müller-Lyer who first described it in 1889, is the different orientation of the two arrowheads. In Western culture people tend to interpret arrowheads that jut out as lengthening something and, vice versa, those pointing inwards as shortening something (Berry 1968). This explanation is supported by a study comparing the response to the Müller-Lyer Illusion by American and Zambian children. The American children were susceptible to the illusion, as were the urban Zambian children, because

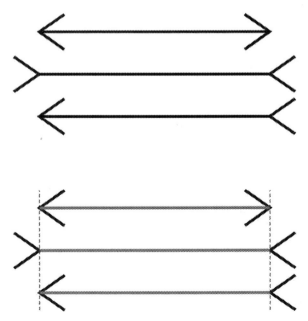

FIGURE 2.1 Müller-Lyer Illusion

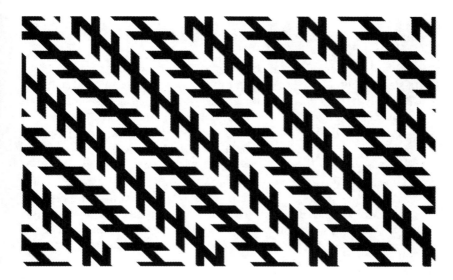

FIGURE 2.2 The Zöllner Illusion

both had been exposed to arrowhead symbols in their upbringing; but this was not the case for the rural Zambian children, who were not (Ahluwalia 1978; see Ninio 2014). The study suggested that exposure to signs and their meanings did indeed affect perception.

An optical illusion that falls into the same category is the Zöllner Illusion, discovered by astrophysicist Johann Zöllner (1860), who stumbled upon a piece of fabric with a design that made parallel lines appear decidedly non-parallel to the eye. The lines presented in Figure 2.2 are parallel, even though they do not seem to be so.

The parallel lines appear slanted because the oblique slashes that cross them in different orientations fool the (Western) mind into interpreting the lines as slanting as well. Again, the illusion suggests that signs influence how we see things. The study of optical illusions implies that relativity effects occur across human systems of representation and expression, not just the linguistic system. For this reason, John Lucy (1997a) has correctly posited that linguistic relativity is really part of a more general *semiotic relativity*—that is, an interrelation between the mind and sign systems (linguistic, visual, gestural, etc.).

Overall, however, the early research on relativity effects was suggestive, rather than definitive. Nevertheless, it established several premises for conducting subsequent research on it:

1. Relativity effects surface at different levels of language, from the lexical and grammatical to the semantic. These vary considerably along a continuum and depend on the language itself.

2. Languages code those aspects of reality that they need (codability); once coded as linguistic categories, these double back on the mind to affect how it views reality.
3. It is not clear whether a specific unit of vocabulary or grammar affects a single mental process (perception, memory, etc.), or a combination.
4. Relativity effects occur in nonverbal systems, such as drawing; and are now considered to be part of a more general semiotic relativity.
5. As the work by Vygotsky showed, there is thought without language, but it has no stability or shape. Preverbal thinking can be seen when infants come into contact with an unknown object. Their first reaction is to explore it with their senses—that is, to handle it, taste it, smell it, listen to any sounds it makes, and visually observe its features. This exploratory phase of knowing is based on instinctive sensory processes. When children learn names for objects, they are subsequently guided by the name of the object to recall it. At that point, language and thought become indistinguishable.
6. Language does not curtail or imprison thought, which can always be modified through creative acts of language. Linguistic relativity simply posits that language and thought become intertwined early in life. So, linguistic relativity should not be confused with linguistic determinism.
7. Endel Tulving (1972) divided memory into episodic and semantic systems. The former specifies and stores past events as episodes. It is useful for recognizing faces, recalling occurrences, and so on. The latter is involved in providing concepts in the form of language and symbolism. The question becomes: Are the two systems interrelated? If so, how so?

As mentioned in Chapter 1, linguistic relativity was seen favorably by many linguists and psychologists in the early decades of the twentieth century, leading to important research on it. However, with the rise of Chomskyan linguistics as a mainstream model of language by the mid-1960s, "linguistic relativity was all but given up for dead," as Wolff and Holmes (2011: 256) aptly put it. Interest was revived in the mid-1980s, dovetailing with the rise and spread of cognitive linguistics and a revival of interest in relativity effects within psychology in the 1990s (Lucy 1996; Imai and Gentner 1997; Lucy and Gaskins 2001). A leader in guiding this new line of inquiry was the American linguist Ronald Langacker (1987, 1990, 1999), who illustrated prolifically that how languages classify their nouns influences how speakers think about their referents and how these affect the grammar of a language. For example, a count noun such as *leaf* in English will be envisioned by a speaker as an outline of a bounded region, whereas a mass noun such as *rice* will be imagined instead as a non-bounded region. This conceptual difference affects the grammar of English. Because bounded referents can be counted, the form *leaf* has a corresponding plural form *leaves*, but *rice* does not. Moreover, *leaf* can be preceded by an indefinite article (*a leaf*), *rice* cannot. Cross-linguistic research has shown how noun classification implies culture-based differences in perception. In Italian, the word corresponding to the English count noun *grapes* is *uva*, which is instead a mass noun. The reason may be that the fruit plays a different role in Italian culture (not only as a fruit, but also as part of wine-making activities). Although this difference does not block understanding, the codability systems in the two languages are different, reflecting different views of the same object.

Three questions that the early period of research on the LRH did not address directly, but which it nevertheless implied are the following:

1. What is the relation of language to the emotions?
2. What can be gleaned from the research on feral children?
3. What is the role of discourse in producing relativity effects?

Few studies have been conducted on question (1) to this day. But there are various findings within early psychology that are suggestive. In the nineteenth century, Hermann Ebbinghaus (1885) gave subjects a list of meaningless syllables to learn by heart, noting how many were remembered after a few minutes, a few hours, and a few days. From these results, he worked out a graph, called the Ebbinghaus curve, which showed how the brain forgets what it had previously stored, discovering that certain factors influence recall—one of these was the emotional meaning attached to forms. This study remains highly suggestive of relativity effects to this day, since it indicates that "felt meaning" is a factor in memory (Kerckhove 2015). A study by Curtiss (1977) of a 13-year-old feral child nicknamed Genie has shed some indirect light on question (2), by extrapolation. Genie was found in 1970 in a room where she had been living alone since the age of 14 months, given food and water through a slit in the door. When discovered, Genie could not speak, and appeared to be puzzled by how words were used. It took intensive instruction to get her to even understand single words. Genie made considerable progress in a relatively short period of time, but she did not reach the levels of language acquisition achieved effortlessly by children who have enjoyed the benefits of a normal cultural upbringing. In 1976, an adolescent boy was found in the forests of Burundi in central Africa. He had been living with monkeys; he walked as a quadruped on his hands and feet; and he climbed trees like an ape (Classen 1991; Candland 1993). The Burundi child, too, was without language, and, like Genie, experienced great difficulty in learning to speak. Significantly, by missing the "critical period" for acquiring language naturally, as it is called in linguistics, the feral children never showed the ability to transcend instinctual forms of interaction. This seems to suggest that language and the mind are interactive agents.

Question (3) was broached somewhat by Boas and Sapir, but it was never really pursued until Hymes' notion of communicative competence made it concretely viable. Sidnell and Enfield (2012: 303) refer to the study of this question as the third phase (or version) of research on linguistic relativity:

> If the first version of the relativity argument emphasizes the consequences of language diversity for the world perceived, the second focuses on the world indexed (and thus produced) in different ways through different languages, in and through the very act of speaking. To these now well-established versions of the relativity argument we want to add a third. The first version began with language conceptualized as a system for thought and the second with speaking as meaningful social behavior. The third version begins with practices of social interaction and the particular forms of social action that they provide for. Our thesis is that different grammatical and lexical patterns of different languages can provide different opportunities for social action.

Many see Russian Mikhail Bakhtin's work in the 1920s (see Bakhtin 1981) and Leo Spitzer's *Stilstudien* (1928) as the starting point for studying the connection between discourse and the psychology of speakers. Decades later, Michel Foucault (1966, 1972) maintained that discourse practices reinforced ideological practices—that is, the way people in authority *talked* about something predisposed people to perceive it as somehow preordained. As Reiner Keller (2011) has since showed, in talking about the world in a certain way, we come to perceive it as somehow the truth of the matter.

Epilogue

The Carrollian poem with which we started this chapter, "Jabberwocky," is an indirect mind experiment in how grammar and meaning are interconnected. Its nonsensical words impel readers to find meanings for them nonetheless, because they resemble the morphological structure of real English words. So, we interpret *toves* as a noun because it has a plural suffix, /-s/, and because it is preceded by the definite article. We perceive *slithy* as an adjective because it appears between an article and a noun, and is constructed with the suffix /-y/. We decode the form *outgrabe* as a verb because it is constructed like the preterite of other English verbs. Through this grammatical assessment, we then infer the potential meanings of the words by connecting them to the narrative of the poem—the slaying of the Jabberwock; and we get a sense of what happens in the poem by imagining what the words could mean.

Carroll's linguistic experiment showed, in sum, that "the morphological traits of the language" and meaning-making are intertwined, as Boas (1911: 23) observed. It was this type of premise that came to the forefront in the early period of research in linguistic anthropology, laying the ground for the LRH to emerge as a principle of language, as will be discussed in Chapter 3. The main premise in the era was that languages are carriers of specific cultural experiences. Linguists such as Boas and Sapir had in effect retrieved the Humboldtian view of an "interdependence" between thought and language examining its validity through specific methods such as fieldwork and ethnography. These have remained central in linguistic anthropology to this day.

Discussion Questions and Activities

Chapter Questions

1. What does it mean to assert that a specific language is tied to the particular experiences of a culture?
2. Does language and thought form a continuum?
3. How was the language-thought-culture nexus researched initially?

Related Questions

4. Linguistic relativity is now seen as part of a more general semiotic relativity. Can you give an example of relativity effects that are not based on language?
5. How could linguistic relativity be rephrased to encompass this broader view?
6. Do you know of similar artificial languages to Jabberwocky? If so, what implications can be gleaned from them in terms of the LRH?
7. How would you encapsulate the ideas of Boas, Sapir, and Vygotsky with respect to the LRH?
8. What kind of experiment could be devised as a follow-up on the one undertaken by Carmichael, Hogan, and Walter that might corroborate their findings? How would you conduct the experiment?

Activities

1. If you know another language, translate or paraphrase the following English concepts into that language:
   (a) sky
   (b) child
   (c) blue
   (d) love
   (e) justice.

   What conceptual-cultural differences do you detect (if any) in the translations?

2. Point out the semantic differences between the words in the following pairs, indicating what they imply and whether these might occur in any other language you know. For example, in the pair *wash-clean*, *wash* means to remove dirt from something using water or some other liquid, whereas *clean* means to remove dirt, with or without water. If you know another language is this difference encoded or not?
   (a) blue–celeste
   (b) table–desk
   (c) chair–sofa
   (d) grape–grapes
   (e) leg–foot.

3. One way to assess the validity of the LRH is to look at mass nouns (nouns that have only a singular form) and attempt to explain why they denote substances or concepts that are perceived to be indivisible or non-countable. Why do you think the following nouns are classified as mass in English, even though they may not be classified in this way in other languages? Give, moreover, any word or phrase that can be used to specify singularity in each case.

   For example, the noun *rice* is classified as mass in English probably because of the large quantity of grains that make up a dish of rice, making counting impracticable. English uses the word *grain* if counting is required: *one grain, two grains*, and so on:
   (a) information
   (b) spinach
   (c) admiration
   (d) clothing
   (e) education
   (f) envy
   (g) gossip.

4. If you know another language, how would the nouns given in Question 3 be translated or paraphrased into it? Do these produce mass nouns as well? If not, explain the relevant translations in grammatical and semantic terms?

5. In how many ways can the following ideas be lexicalized in English (rendered as lexemes or other lexical structures)? What does this tell us potentially about English-speaking cultures?
   (a) a flying creature
   (b) a close relative
   (c) types of liquid
   (d) needs
   (e) anger.
6. Make up your own Jabberwock-type words. Explain what meanings they may suggest.

3
THE WHORFIAN HYPOTHESIS

Prologue

Benjamin Lee Whorf became a major figure studying linguistic relativity in the 1930s—a term that he himself coined (Chapter 1). He graduated from MIT in 1918 in chemical engineering, and started working right after as a fire prevention inspector for the Hartford Fire Insurance Company. In one incident, during his time as an inspector, Whorf noticed that a firm had labeled a bunch of gasoline drums as *empty* (Whorf 1956: 134–159). As a chemical engineer, he realized that the drums were full of gasoline vapor, making them highly flammable, although he noticed that the workers did not handle them carefully, even smoking in the room with the empty drums, but not in the room with the full ones. Whorf concluded that by habitually speaking of the vapor-filled drums as *empty*, the workers came to perceive them as inert, being oblivious to the risks posed by smoking near them. The incident became both a key anecdote for both the supporters and critics of linguistic relativity (Edwards 1991, 1994).

Apparently inspired by this event, Whorf enrolled at Yale University shortly thereafter to study linguistics with Edward Sapir. It was Sapir's courses that influenced Whorf to study the relation between language and thought. He became particularly interested in the Hopi language and how different it was from what he called Standard Average European (SAE) languages. Whorf died very young from cancer in 1941, leaving many of his works to be published posthumously (Whorf 1956). In homage to his contributions the linguistic relativity hypothesis was renamed the Sapir-Whorf Hypothesis in the 1950s (Hoijer 1954), abbreviated a little later to the Whorfian Hypothesis (WH). As mentioned previously, in the 1960s, the WH fell out of favor, as linguistics veered towards the Chomskyan model of language, with critics even attributing to Whorf ideas he had never expressed. However, starting in the 1990s, interest in the WH was reignited, as new research came forward to provide intriguing support for it (Boroditsky 2001, 2003; Levinson and Brown 1994; Levinson and Jaisson 2006; Levinson and Wilkins 2006). Some of this research will be discussed in this chapter.

To discuss the research, it might be useful to adopt the device of a scale, called a Whorfian Scale, on which relativity effects would range from 0—no relativity effects—to 1 for maximum relativity effects:

0 (No relativity) ——————————— 1 (Maximum relativity)

Whorfian Scale

So, the closer a concept framed in a language is to 1, the less cross-linguistic codability it would have; the closer it is to 0, the more codability. The degree of codability can be accessed via the usual methods for assessing the LRH, such as translation—concepts that are hard to translate would fall near 1 and those that are easily translatable would fall near 0. For instance, the Italian word *simpatico*, which does not have a single lexical equivalent in English, although it can be rendered with paraphrases and approximations, would fall near 1, since its meaning can never be completely captured in English. On the other hand, a word such as *auto* in Italian coincides with English *automobile*. It can thus be located near 0 on the Whorfian Scale. This is just a convenient way for relating codability and relativity effects to each other. It is not a precise mathematical instrument.

This chapter will deal with the WH and the kinds of general research studies based on it. It will also discuss critiques of the WH. The three main questions that will be addressed are:

1. Do languages truly shape how their speakers actually think?
2. What kinds of proof would be required to test the WH to any degree of psychological realism?
3. What valid counterarguments can be made against the WH?

The Hopi Language

While at Yale, Whorf became fascinated with the Mesoamerican and Uto-Aztecan languages of Central America and western North America. As a result, he carried out fieldwork in various parts of Mexico, collecting data on the indigenous languages of the region. As Sapir's student, he had developed a special interest in the Hopi language, deciding to enroll in a program of graduate studies to pursue this interest, which however he never completed.

Sapir had a profound impact on Whorf, influencing how he came to view the relation between language and thought, even though Sapir had himself become influenced at the time by logical positivistic views such as those of Bertrand Russell (1921) and Ludwig Wittgenstein (1921). But this did not completely pull him away from his relativistic standpoint. It seems that Sapir came to believe that relativity effects could be tamed (in a manner of speaking) through the employment language according to the laws of logic. Nonetheless, Sapir encouraged Whorf to look at the relation of language to thought encouraging him to study the Uto-Aztecan languages as a means to compare them to SAE languages. Whorf decided to focus on the Hopi language, working with a speaker of Hopi living in Manhattan, New York City. In 1938, he took a short field trip to a village on the Hopi Reservation in Arizona, in order to complete the ethnographic account of the language that he had developed from his informant in New York City.

> **THE HOPI LANGUAGE**
>
> Hopi is an Uto-Aztecan language spoken mainly in north-eastern Arizona. Younger generations of Hopi are now primarily English-speaking. Despite the apparent decline, many children are being reared in the language in an effort to preserve it. In his fieldwork, Whorf identified four dialects: (1) First Mesa (Polacca); (2) Mishongnovi (Toreva); (3) Shipaulovi; and (4) Third Mesa (Oraibi).

Whorf's analysis of how the Hopi language marked time led him to formulate the principle of linguistic relativity, which he saw as a linguistic counterpart physical relativity theory, as discussed previously, and especially the notion of *spacetime* as a unified entity. SAE languages separate the two—space and time—linguistically and conceptually, with nouns typically referring to spatial entities as locations and verbs to actions and events as unfolding in terms of a tripartite linear division of time into *past*, *present*, and *future*. Whorf discovered that the Hopi language does not mark spatial and temporal events as distinctive conceptual structures, but, rather, as part of spacetime as a unified entity. For this reason, Whorf called Hopi a *timeless* language—a controversial term that led to various critiques, as we shall see. But what he meant with the term was, essentially, that Hopi verbs do not mark time in a linear fashion, allowing speakers to validate their intents with respect to temporal events (Whorf 1941: 231):

> The timeless Hopi verb does not distinguish between the present, past, and future of the event itself but must always indicate what type

of validity the speaker intends the statement to have: (1) report of an event; (2) expectation of an event; (3) generalization or law about events. Where the speaker and listener are in contact with the same objective field, [it] is divided by our language into the two conditions, which it calls present and past, respectively. This division is unnecessary for a language which assures one that the statement is a report. Hopi grammar, by means of its forms called aspects and modes, also makes it easy to distinguish among momentary, continued, and repeated occurrences, and to indicate the actual sequence of reported events. Thus the universe can be described without recourse to a concept of dimensional time.

Whorf identified three main aspects of Hopi verbs, which he named as follows:

1. *Reportive:* This is the default form of the verb, allowing the speaker to assert that an event has occurred or is still occurring.
2. *Expective:* This implies that something is about to happen; it is marked with the verbal suffix /-ni/.
3. *Nomic:* This refers to some general truth contained in the verb's meaning; it is marked with the suffix /-ŋʷi/.

Accompanying these aspects, there are subclasses of adverbials, which Whorf (1946) called *temporals* and *tensors*, which allow for reference to spatial locations in time. Whorf claimed that, by not seeing time as an objectifiable phenomenon, Hopi people are less dependent on devices such as watches, timetables, and the like to carry out their daily affairs. The Hopi language does not even have a specific word for *time*, because it is not needed (Whorf 1956: 57):

> I find it gratuitous to assume that a Hopi who knows only the Hopi language and the cultural ideas of his own society has the same notions, often supposed to be intuitions, of time and space as we have, and that are generally assumed to be universal. In particular he has no notion or intuition of time as a smooth flowing continuum in which everything in the universe proceeds at an equal rate, out of a future into a present and into a past. After a long and careful analysis the Hopi language is seen to contain no words, grammatical forms, construction or expressions that refer directly to what we call "time", or to past, present or future.

Overall, Hopi grammar treats time as a cyclical, rather than a linear phenomenon, as does SAE. This influences all other domains of grammar. So, instead of saying *five days*, a Hopi speaker would say *on the fifth day* indicating that something occurs in a cycle not in a line. This cyclical aspect of grammar mirrors the Hopi worldview of history as a repeating process.

As discussed, Whorf was influenced by Einstein's theory of relativity (Lee 1996). And this is the reason why he adopted the term *linguistic relativity* to describe language, reflecting the idea of the different but equally valid interpretations of physical reality by different observers due to differences in their physical circumstances (Einstein) or their linguistic circumstances (Whorf). In retrospect, Whorf's ideas actually have resonance in physics itself, given that relativity physics is not based on a direct observation of the world, but on an interpretation of the world in terms of a mathematical language that allows for this interpretation to become concrete. As Whorf suggested, the Hopi verb system would have actually been better suited for describing physical relativity phenomena, since the concept of spacetime as conceptualized by physicists is implicit in it.

Classical mechanics was influenced by the linguistic structures of SAE languages, which characterize time and space as discrete entities. This led to the assumption that physical laws should look the same no matter in which direction one looks—that is, the laws are *invariant*. But what happens if there is a universe where this invariance does not hold? It would be unimaginable, because SAE does not have any linguistic device to envision it. As Lee Smolin (2013) asserts, in the seventeenth century, scientists wondered whether "the world is in essence mathematical or it lives in time." He then goes on to assert that "Einstein's two theories of relativity are, at their most basic, theories of time—or, better, timelessness." This is the likely reason why Whorf concluded that timelessness is inherent in Hopi, paralleling the physicist's model of the universe.

Whorf died in 1941, but his ideas became discussed and debated throughout the 1940s, 1950s, and 1960s. However, because of their intuitive appeal, they sometimes led to exaggerations and even misrepresentations. For example, in 1958 Stuart Chase maintained that the WH implied that the Hopi were in a better frame of mind to grasp the physical concept of time as a fourth dimension, which Whorf had never asserted. In a 1964 work, John Greenway made the following remark: "You have a watch, because Americans are obsessed with time. If you were a Hopi, you would have none, the Hopi have no concept of time." And in 1971, Euler and Dobyns claimed that "The English concept of time is nearly incomprehensible to the Hopi." These were misrepresentations of the WH.

Critical Reactions

One of the first serious critiques of the WH came from philosopher Max Black in 1959, who argued that it is refuted by the simple reason that Hopi concepts can be translated into English, even when there are no exact correspondences between the words and phrases in the two languages. But, using the Whorfian Scale, this critique can be attenuated by the fact that the degree of translatability relates to the degree of codability. In the area of verbal time, the WH would simply assert that the degree of codability between Hopi and SAE is near the untranslatable end. A similar type of critique was that of Helmut Gipper (1972), who decided to conduct his own fieldwork among the Hopi. He claimed that German and Hopi have essentially the same understanding of time, albeit by different verbal means. So, distinctions between, say, past and present, which are encoded explicitly in German verbs with suffixes, are rendered equivalently by Hopi linguistic categories such as those identified by Whorf. Gipper showed this by simply translating Hopi phrases into German, noting that little was lost in the translation.

The first comprehensive critique of Whorf's treatment of Hopi time came a little later from one of Gipper's students, Ekkehart Malotki (1983) (Chapter 1). Malotki carried out his own ethnographic fieldwork with speakers of the Third Mesa dialect. He found that in certain situations, and unlike what Whorf believed, the Hopi do indeed count days in a similar manner—they do so with compound words, such as *payistala* ("the third day of a ceremony"), which is composed of the morphemes *paayo* ("three"), /-s-/ ("times"), and *taala* ("daylight"), meaning literally "three-times-day." After examining Whorf's categories (reportive, expective, nomic), Malotki claimed that the suffix /-ni/ was an actual marker of future time, and /-ŋʷi/ a marker of habitual actions (similar to the imperfect tenses in SAE). He also countered Whorf's analysis of Hopi adverbials, indicating that the language has specific adverbs, as in SAE, for indicating distance in space and in time. For example, the lexeme *ep* means both "there" and "then."

Malotki's book was reviewed by Bernard Comrie (1984), who agreed with Malotki that Hopi did indeed mark time in its verb system as did SAE, but which it had simply codified differently. But Comrie also noted that Malotki himself was misguided in claiming that the Hopi language had a tense system based on the opposition of future-versus-non-future. Comrie suggested that the opposition is a modal rather than temporal one, implying that Hopi has no tense distinction in this case, thus supporting Whorf. Goddard and Wierzbicka (2002) also reviewed Malotki's data a little later, concluding that the Hopi language had the same "semantic primes" of other languages, which it encoded differently. Semantic primes are concepts that cannot be defined absolutely. For instance, although the meaning of "touching" is readily understood, defining it involves other words or phrases that end up taking us back to the concept itself.

The critiques by Black, Gipper, Malotki, and others are based essentially on different interpretations of Whorf's analysis of Hopi grammar. At the very least, they have been useful as part of a larger debate on the LRH, showing that translatability and codability are interrelated, as the

Whorfian Scale device is intended to make evident. But the critiques by linguists who espouse the universalist (Chomskyan) paradigm, such as Steven Pinker (1994, 2007) and John McWhorter (2009, 2016), have been unnecessarily acerbic, even characterizing Whorf as an incompetent linguist who had no significant understanding of linguistics. Pinker simply dismissed Whorf outright with his notion of "mentalese"(Pinker 1994: 60)—a notion that was put forth originally by Jerry Fodor (1975). Fodor saw the mind as a processor of abstract symbols. Because these manifest themselves in discourse, serving thought during speech, he referred to them as mental representations that are similar to the algorithms used to write computer programs. Cumulatively, they constitute the brain's "language of thought." But the irony is that the terms *mentalese* and *language of thought* allude to linguistic ideas forming in the brain, thus indirectly corroborating the WH, which simply connects language and thought without any intervening (and irrelevant) construct. Pinker (1994) also dismissed Whorf's anecdote about the *empty* label (above) as nonsense. Pinker simply ridiculed the gas drum anecdote as a failing in human insight rather than language. But, as Lucy (1997b) subsequently argued, the interpretive effect produced by the label *empty* cannot be so easily dismissed, since by changing labels a different understanding of the situation would ensue.

As discussed briefly in Chapter 1, Whorf's statement about the many terms for *snow* in Native American languages was also assailed strongly by the same group of linguists (McWhorter 2016; Pullum 1991). Even though English does not have distinct lexical items as those mentioned by Whorf (Chapter 1), the critics pointed out that it can render the same concepts through paraphrases or lexical equivalents, such as *hail, sleet, ice, icicle, slush*, and *snowflake*. It was actually Boas (1911: 25–26) who first made reference to Inuktitut (an Inuit language) having multiple words for snow:

> To take again the example of English, we find that the idea of *water* is expressed in a great variety of forms: one term serves to express *water* as a *liquid*; another one, *water* in the form of a large expanse (*lake*); others, *water* as running in a large body or in a small body (*river* and *brook*); still other terms express *water* in the form of *rain, dew, wave*, and *foam*. It is perfectly conceivable that this variety of ideas, each of which is expressed by a single independent term in English, might be expressed in other languages by derivations from the same term. Another example of the same kind, the words for *snow* in [Inuktitut], may be given. Here we find one word, *aput*, expressing snow on the ground; another one, *qana*, falling snow; a third one, *piqsirpoq*, drifting snow; and a fourth one, *qimuqsuq*, a snowdrift.

Now, the question becomes: Do speakers of languages that have specific lexemes for snow, perceive snow events and situations differently? Whorf answered this question rather insightfully, albeit indirectly. He argued that speakers of Inuit languages may look at a winter landscape and differentiate *aniu* ("snow for making water") from *masak* ("wet snow"), whereas English speakers would "see" the same landscape as having plain *snow*. This observation does not preclude the fact that the Inuit words are in effect translatable. But they would occur near the low codability end of the Whorfian Scale, which means that the meanings of the Inuit words are not so easily captured by translation, especially when we go beyond the realm of literal meaning into the realm of metaphor and connotative meaning.

The last statement requires some commentary here, even though the topic of metaphor will be taken up subsequently. Take, as an example, the word *blue* in English. Its coinage was probably motivated from observing a pattern of hue found in natural phenomena such as the sky and the sea, and then by then noting the occurrence of the same hue in other things. The specific concept that the word *blue* elicits in the mind will, of course, be different from language to language and from individual to individual. But, as we shall see, the same hue range is covered by different lexemes in some languages or an analogous one in other languages. This type of meaning occurs at the literal level. However, when speakers use the very same word to characterize emotions and other abstractions, the level of meaning changes radically:

1. Today I've got the *blues*.
2. The news hit me right out of the *blue*.

The use of *blue* in example (1) to mean "sad" or "gloomy" is tied to culture-specific semantics, coming out of the tradition of blues music, which is perceived typically to evoke sadness or melancholy through its melodies, harmonies, rhythms, and lyrics. The use of *blue* in example (2) to render the concept of "unexpectedness" comes, instead, from the tradition of ascribing unpredictability to the weather. In other words, the "thoughts" encoded by *blue* in these examples involve metaphorical or connotative meaning (Chapter 6). Metaphorical concepts are almost always closer to 1 on the Whorfian Scale than are literal ones. The latter can be rendered easily by translation or paraphrase; the former cannot. The point is that countering the WH by using translation as proof of its invalidity ignores how language reaches beyond literal meaning.

Resurgence of Interest

Whorf's ideas started gaining a resurgence of interest in the 1990s. For example, Lucy (1992b: 63) argued that Malotki failed to acknowledge that Whorf's notion of timelessness simply asserted that Hopi structures the perception of time differently than does English grammar, not that it lacks time markers in it. In 1991, Penny Lee (1996) argued that Malotki's critique that Whorf's categories did not capture the essence of the distinction between verbal tenses and adverbials in Hopi. Lee also pointed out that the critiques of the WH were motivated by innatist theories, not by objective analysis. In the same year, Gumperz and Levinson (1996) put together a volume of research papers that subsequently kindled great interest in the WH, especially within linguistic anthropology, culminating in David Dinwoodie's (2006) revisitation of Malotki, providing examples that he had gathered ethnographically of how Hopi speakers explain events not in discrete categories, but in terms of cycles of nature.

The advent of cognitive linguistics, spearheaded by linguist George Lakoff (Lakoff 1987; Lakoff and Johnson 1999), was also a major factor in the resurgence of interest in the WH. In his 1987 book, *Women, Fire, and Dangerous Things*, Lakoff asserted that Whorf had been on the right track all along in claiming that differences in grammatical and lexical categories were the source of differences in perception, cognition, memory, and overall worldview. The implication was that certain relativity effects involve perception (as the various terms for *snow* could indicate), cognition (as different verb categories for codifying time may imply), or memory (as the Carmichael, Hogan, and Walter study described in Chapter 2 showed).

RELEVANT NOTIONS IN A WHORFIAN FRAMEWORK

Perception: Processing sensory information via language and other semiotic systems.

Cognition: The process of understanding as revealed in linguistic categories.

Memory: The process of recalling and re-interpreting information via linguistic labels and structures.

Thought: The process of encompassing all three above—perceiving, cognizing, and recalling holistically. The term *Gestalt* is sometimes used to refer to this amalgamation.

Worldview: A particular conception of reality shaped by the semiotic systems acquired in childhood.

Many of these processes can be considered aspects of mental perspective. Consider English expressions such as *in front of* or *ahead*, with which we imply that something will occur in the future, while something that is *behind us* is perceived as having occurred in the past.

1. Your whole life lies *in front* of you.
2. Do you know what lies *ahead*?
3. Just put all that *behind* you. It's ancient history.
4. I have fallen *behind* in my work.

What do these imply in terms of mental perspective? The plausible answer is that they indicate that English speakers perceive time as something that occurs on a linear path, with the past *behind* and the future *ahead*. For Greek speakers, this linear relation has been encoded differently. In Greek, the future is marked as being *behind* and the past as *in front* on the timeline. Now, the expressions above suggest that English speakers perceive time as standing still while people travel through it, from left to right. Greek speakers, on the other hand, perceive the future as not yet visible, while the past is already in front, and thus visible.

A well-known study on the connection between a specific aspect of grammar and its effects on mental perspective is the one by a government survey-taker, Alfred Bloom (1981), who conducted surveys just before Hong Kong became part of China in the early 1980s, gaining autonomy from its British past. During a survey, he found the answer to one of his questions intriguing: *If the government were to take away your freedom, what would you do?* He discovered that native speakers of English responded with answers such as the following (paraphrased here, for convenience):

SPEAKER A: I would leave.
SPEAKER B: I'm not sure what I would do.
SPEAKER C: I probably wouldn't do anything.
SPEAKER D: I would organize a protest.
SPEAKER E: What could I do? Probably nothing.

Bloom's question is an example of a counterfactual, a syntactic form that is intended to convey the concept of "contrary to given facts." In all responses by native speakers, the question elicited a type of response that follows logically from the counterfactual. However, when he asked the same question to speakers who had learned English in school and for whom it was not a native language, he received the following typical response:

QUESTION: If the government were to take away your freedom, what would you do?
RESPONSE: It hasn't.

Bloom explained the variation in the pattern of responses in Whorfian terms by suggesting that the non-native speakers had not learned counterfactuals and thus answered his question in factual terms. Bloom's study created some controversy (Au 1984; Cheng 2013). But others saw it differently, namely, as simply documenting a relativity effect of grammar on mental perspective.

Research on the relation between language and mental perspective gained momentum in the 1990s. The classic study of Navajo children reported by Claire Kramsch (1998: 13–14) is a typical example. Navajo encodes the actions of "picking up a round object," such as a ball, and "picking up a long, thin flexible object," such as a rope, as obligatory linguistic categories. In one experiment, when presented with a blue rope and asked to choose either a yellow rope or a blue stick to match the blue rope, Navajo children tended to choose the yellow rope, associating the object chosen on the basis of shape, whereas English-speaking children almost always chose the blue stick, selecting the object on the basis of color, even though both groups of children were perfectly able to distinguish colors and shapes. Interestingly, Navajo children who had studied English chose the blue stick and yellow rope in a fairly equal way.

Some truly fascinating work on the WH was subsequently conducted by John Lucy (Lucy 2014; Lucy and Gaskins 2001, 2003) and Lera Boroditsky (2000, 2001, 2003, Boroditsky, Schmidt, and Phillips 2003). Lucy's work on the Yucatec language is particularly relevant; it was mentioned in Chapter 2 but is worth revisiting here rapidly.

YUCATEC

Yucatec is the Native language spoken in south-eastern Mexico, at the northern tip of the Yucatán Peninsula. It is a Mayan language—the Yucatec word *mayab* meaning "flat" is the source of the word *Maya*. After the Spanish conquest of the region, the area became Spanish-speaking, but has retained its linguistic heritage through several educational campaigns. Like Hopi, the Yucatec perspective of time is delivered by linguistic categories that are different from those in SAE languages. Temporal perspective is often shaped by the pragmatic context in which a speech act occurs.

English and Yucatec differ systematically in the ways in which they mark the number (singular-plural) of nouns referring to a stable object (for example, *candle*) and to those referring to a pliable object (for example, *clay*): English requires a morpheme, such as /-s/, to indicate multiple stable objects (*candles*), but not pliable ones (*clay*). Yucatec does not mark the plural of nouns referring to stable objects and, like English, also leaves the number of pliable objects unmarked. In one experiment, Lucy (2014) found that in recognition and recall tasks English speakers attended to the number of stable objects, Yucatec speakers did not, marking other aspects of the object's appearance instead. However, in the case of pliable objects, where the two languages coincide, the speakers showed no differences. Lucy concluded that the specific number marking systems predicted specific cognitive and memory responses.

In several works with Suzanne Gaskins (Lucy and Gaskins, 2001, 2003), Lucy has also investigated how children of different language backgrounds shared various cognitive traits before they reached the age of nine; differences emerged by that age, when they started speaking and thinking in a different way and in line with the adult speakers of their language. The implication is that relativity effects crystallize gradually as the child gains increasing control over the native language. It is relevant to note that Lucy has also studied relativity effects in second-language learning (Chapter 5)—an oft neglected area of research with respect to the WH.

Boroditsky has focused on how relativity effects influence behavior in specific contexts of speech interaction. For example, metaphorical concepts of time predispose speakers to envision it in specific perspectival ways. As discussed, English speakers think of the movement of time as linear—that is, as analogous to their conception of spatial horizontal movement. On the other hand, Mandarin speakers associate it with vertical movement (Boroditsky 2001). So, a paraphrase of *time marches on* in Mandarin may be *time goes up*. She suggests, however, that these differences do not block cross-cultural understanding. Therefore, native tongues may have an effect on the mind, but it is not a deterministic one.

Sound Symbolism

In addition to the spate of comparative studies of the effects of the grammar and the lexicon on mental perspective that started in the 1990s and still continue today, work on sound symbolism theory has emerged as highly supportive of the WH. It is worthwhile revisiting this theory briefly here, since it has received relatively little attention within the framework of the WH, and especially since Whorf himself saw it as an important aspect of linguistic relativity (Whorf 1956). *Sound symbolism* refers to the representation or the evocation of the sense of a word by its phonetic structure. It was von Humboldt (1836) who was among the first to envision a connection between the phonetic structure of words and their meanings. But, even before Humboldt, ancient philosophers linked vocal sound, writing characters, and meaning speculatively. For instance, in ancient Chinese writings, as Schuessler (2007) points out, words with /m/ were associated with something black, those made up of /n/ with something soft or flexible, and those with /k/ with some abrupt action. In Plato's *Cratylus* dialogue (Plato 2013), Socrates suggests that words are originally constructed with sounds that reflect some property of their referents. However, the many counter-examples given to Socrates by his interlocutor, Hermogenes, led Socrates to admit that his view was, after all, highly speculative. In the seventeenth century, John Locke (1690) dismissed such speculation outright, pointing out that if sound symbolism were a principle of language, then we would all be speaking the same language. He maintained that the relation between words and their phonetic structure is arbitrary, with only a few onomatopoeic exceptions, as did Saussure (1916) subsequently.

The systematic investigation of sound symbolism started in the 1920s (for example, Jespersen 1922). In the 1950s, Morris Swadesh (1951, 1955, 1959, 1971) championed it as a major principle of language design, drawing attention to the fact that most of the world's languages used it in the formation of their words and even in the constitution of their grammatical categories. For instance, he argued that front vowels (/i/-type and /e/-type vowels) are used commonly to construct words in which "nearness" was implied, in contrast to back vowels (/a/-type, /o/-type, and /u/-type vowels), which are used instead to construct words in which the opposite concept of "distance" was implied—in English, common examples are *here* versus *there*, *near* versus *far*, and *this* versus *that*. Around the same time, Brown, Black, and Horowitz (1955) discussed experiments that seemed to substantiate Swadesh's claims. For instance, in one experiment speakers of English listened to pairs of antonyms from a language unrelated to English and were then asked to guess, given English equivalents, which English word translated which foreign word. For instance, when asked to match the Chinese words *ch'ing* and *chung* to English equivalents *light* and *heavy*, not necessarily in that order, it was found that most English speakers matched *ch'ing* to *light* and *chung* to *heavy* correctly. A little later, Brown (1958) gave the example of Samoan *ongololo* referring to "centipede" as an example of how the syllables in a word correspond to the number of distinct elements in the sound, object, or action. Interestingly, in Chinese, sound symbolic modeling pertains to the feelings that shapes evoke. This is why some Chinese classifiers (words indicating semantic category) are based on shape, such as morphemes that indicate long, flat, and round objects, containers, pairs, and sets.

Margaret Magnus (1999) amassed a significant corpus of data to show that words constructed with the same or equivalent phonemic categories tend to coalesce around a similar core of meanings. Magnus identifies four basic sound-symbolic processes:

1. *Onomatopoeia*: refers to a straightforward, intentional imitation of sound properties: *splash, pop, bang*.
2. *Clustering*: refers to words that share a phoneme cluster around a referential domain; so, if /h/ is used for *house*, then a disproportionate

amount of words will start with /h/ within the same lexical field: *hut, home, hovel, habitat.*
3. *Iconism* refers to words that have similar or analogous referents. For instance, words such as *stomp, tramp,* and *step* show the phonemic pattern of /m/ + /p/ and /s/ + /t/, sharing semantic linkages.
4. *Phenomimes* and *psychomimes* are "quasi onomatopoeic" words; the former evoke latent sound reference and the latter psychological states. The word *duck* is a phenomine because it suggests the sound made by a "duck," already encoded onomatopoeically with *quack*. *Ugh* is a psychomime that represents some inner state indirectly.

Whorf himself had suggested that sound symbolism is so deeply rooted in our minds that we hardly ever notice that it guides our interpretation of the meaning of reality. He put it thus (Whorf 1956: 267–268):

> In the psychological experiments, human subjects seem to associate the experiences of bright, cold, sharp, hard, high, light (in weight), quick, high-pitched, narrow, and so on in a long series, with each other; and conversely, the experiences of dark, warm, yielding, soft, blunt, low, heavy, slow, low-pitched, wide, etc. in another long series. This occurs whether the words for such associated experiences resemble them or not, but the ordinary person is likely to perceive a relation to words only when it is a relation of likenesses to such a series in the vowels and consonants of words.

Epilogue

We started the chapter alluding to the well-known anecdote concerning the label *empty* on gasoline drums, which influenced the employees at the company to perceive them as safe when, in reality, they were highly flammable and thus dangerous. That observation encapsulates the main premise of the WH in microcosm—language influences perception. The influence takes the form of relativity effects, from more to less, stronger to weaker, falling on what has been called a Whorfian Scale here. Aware of the possibility that his anecdote may be misconstrued, Whorf wrote the following to an editor (cited in Lee 1996: 153):

> I have thought of possibly adding a brief statement or a footnote saying that I don't wish to imply that language is the sole or even the leading factor in the types of behaviour mentioned such as the fire-causing carelessness through misunderstandings induced by language, but that this is simply a coordinate factor along with others. It didn't

seem at first that this should be necessary if the reader uses ordinary common sense.

Whorf's work on the Hopi language convinced him that it would be misguided to see language simply as a means to label the world arbitrarily. When we acquire a particular language in childhood, its specific linguistic features become habits of mind. Enfield (2015: 209–210) puts it as follows:

> Here is what Whorf suggested. When deciding how to behave, one might naturally use language in thinking, and in so doing one may effectively discard, or fail to notice, important information that happens not to feature in a linguistic rendering of the state of affairs at hand. It is not that people cannot comprehend alternative depictions of reality. Nor is it that we cannot think without language. It is that we are creatures of habit. If language is our most practiced resource, it should be no surprise that language instills deep cognitive habits: habits of attention and disattention, habits of reasoning—or failing to reason—in deciding how to act.

The resurgence in research on the WH in the last few decades has largely corroborated Whorf's main claim that language does not just provide convenient labels for naming things, it also shapes how speakers view or interpret the world with those labels. Consider again the example of a "device for keeping track of time," mentioned briefly in Chapter 1. Given that it is a human-made object, there really should be little or no variation in the ways different languages refer to it. But there is. As discussed, English has two words for this device, *clock* and *watch*. This double classification has a historical motivation. The word *watch* appeared in northern Europe several centuries ago when people started strapping timepieces around their wrists, so that they could literally "watch" time in order to carry out tasks or maintain appointments with precision. As the psychologist Robert Levine (1997) suggests, a fixation with being "precisely on time" is typical of cultures that distinguish between *clocks* and *watches*, but less so of others that do not. As he indicates, Burmese monks know more or less that it is time to get up in the morning when there is enough light to see the veins in their hands. They are not as compulsive about precise time-keeping as most modern people are, thus avoiding many of the stress-related syndromes that afflict us in the West.

The WH also raises significant questions about the relation between language and social roles. In English, terms such as *chairman*, *spokesman*, and so on are cited as examples of how the English language has predisposed its users to view certain social roles in gender terms. By changing the words we alter the way we *think* about roles. This has actually transpired as words such as those above, marked with the /-man/ suffix, have been replaced with words such as *chairperson* (or simply *chair*) and *spokesperson*.

The WH also raises important questions related to the manipulation of mind with language. As George Orwell showed in his 1949 novel *Nineteen Eighty-Four*, the fictional language of a totalitarian world, which he called Newspeak, was used by the leaders of that world to control thought and thus to induce orthodoxy, as the character Syme discusses in the novel (Orwell 1949: 918):

> By 2050—earlier, probably—all real knowledge of Oldspeak will have disappeared. The whole literature of the past will have been destroyed. Chaucer, Shakespeare, Milton, Byron—they'll exist only in Newspeak versions, not merely changed into something different, but actually contradictory of what they used to be. Even the literature of The Party will change. Even the slogans will change. How could you have a slogan like Freedom is Slavery when the concept of freedom has been abolished? The whole climate of thought will be different. In fact, there will be no thought, as we understand it now. Orthodoxy means not thinking—not needing to think. Orthodoxy is unconsciousness.

In sum, the WH is hardly a trivial idea, as some linguists have sustained. At the very least, it can be used as a theoretical construct, not only to examine the effects of grammar and vocabulary on mental perspective, but also on how language can be used to shape the mind, for better or worse, as Orwell certainly knew.

Discussion Questions and Activities

Chapter Questions

1. Do languages truly shape how their speakers actually think?
2. What kinds of proof would be required to test the WH to any degree of psychological realism?
3. What valid counterarguments can be made against the WH?

Related Questions

4. Do you agree with Whorf that a label such as *empty* can lead to an incorrect perception of a situation? Can you think of other examples that may lead people astray in a similar fashion?

5. Boas and Whorf have been attacked for suggesting that the multiple lexical forms for referring to *snow* in Inuit languages reveal how speakers view the reality of snow differently. What are the main counterarguments? Can these counterarguments be refuted?
6. What differentiates the Whorfian Hypothesis from previous views of linguistic relativity?
7. Does the Whorfian Hypothesis have any insights to offer on how people use language to lie and manipulate minds? Can the phenomenon of fake news be connected to the WH? If so, how so?
8. Words clearly affect emotional responses. If the WH is valid, this would suggest that emotions are experienced differently in different cultures. Is this plausible? If so, how so?

Activities

1. If you know another language, indicate the forms (words, phrases, etc.) that are used to refer to the following, comparing them to English and indicating whether the differences could be a source of relativity effects:
   (a) snow
   (b) seal
   (c) present
   (d) past
   (e) future.
2. The following largely antiquated terms and expressions use *man*. What terms are currently used (or should be used, if there are none) in their place to eliminate the gender bias implicit in them?
   (a) fireman
   (b) postman
   (c) mankind
   (d) man and wife
   (e) man-made.
3. The following exemplify some aspect of sound symbolism. Indicate how each connects phonetic structure to meaning. If you know another language, how would you render the same concepts in that language?
   (a) tick-tock
   (b) cock-a-doodle-doo
   (c) Ouch!
   (d) Mmmm, good!
   (e) Oh-oh!

4. Translate the following words in any language you know. Note the differences and what these might imply in Whorfian terms.
   (a) bird
   (b) freedom
   (c) interest
   (d) tree
   (e) sky
   (f) water
   (g) hill
   (h) finger
   (i) head
   (j) need
   (k) love.
5. The difference between denotative (literal) and metaphorical meaning is critical in assessing the WH, as will also be discussed in Chapter 6. Classify the italicized words as having denotative or metaphorical (connotative) meaning in the sentences, specifying what that meaning is:
   (a) I bought a new *home* yesterday.
   (b) *Home* is where the heart is.
   (c) I bought a new *board* to play chess on.
   (d) The *board* met yesterday.
   (e) I do not know all the multiplication *tables*.
   (f) We bought new *tables* for our apartment.
   (g) When you caress me, I always *purr*.
   (h) Our cat almost never *purrs*.

4

VOCABULARY AND GRAMMAR

Prologue

In Shinzwani, a language spoken in the Comoro Islands of the western Indian Ocean, the word for *mother* corresponds to both English *mother* and *aunt* (Ahmed-Chamanga 1992). The plausible reason for this is that the mother figure of Shinzwani culture performs the kinship duties expected of both mothers and aunts in English-speaking culture. This different naming pattern reveals a different organization of kinship relations between the two cultures and, thus, a different understanding of what motherhood entails socially. In an analogous fashion, Italian uses the single word *nipote* in correspondence to both English *nephew/niece* and *grandchild*—a lexical difference that similarly alludes to a difference in the perception of family relations. Such cross-linguistic examples are numerous, showing that even naming kin is not guided by the same understanding of the biology of kinship relations, but rather, that the specific naming systems used reflect socially-based perceptions of kinship and what roles different kin play in social systems. As such, they constitute test cases for investigating the LRH.

The study of vocabulary-based distinctions has, actually, characterized a large portion of research on the LRH—some of which has been described previously. In this framework, the lexicon is seen as much more than an arbitrary collection of names for things; it is seen as constituting a perceptual-cognitive filter for assessing, interpreting, and evaluating the world. The same principle applies to grammar. We have discussed previously how a category such as the plural formation of nouns can differ across languages, revealing differences in recognition and recall. This same pattern connecting differences in grammatical categories to differences in cognitive-perceptual frames of mind can be found across the entire domain of grammar.

This chapter looks at the type of work on vocabulary and grammar aimed at testing the LRH. It will focus on kinship and color terms, since these have generated a large amount of research and debate. The specific questions that will guide the present discussion are:

1. Among cultures, do differences in vocabulary and grammar entail differences in cultural organization and thus of understanding?
2. What can we learn about linguistic relativity from studying kinship and color terms?
3. Are habits of mind equivalent to habits of language?

Specialized Vocabulary

A central theme in the work of Franz Boas was that words are not arbitrary labels for naming the world (Chapter 2). Rather, they serve the specific classificatory (taxonomic) functions required by different cultures, encoding realities that are perceived to be critical by them—geographical, environmental, psychological, and so on. For example, the Papago people of Arizona have devised four classes of lexemes for referring to plants that reflect the reality of living in the desert (Mathiot 1962):

1. Trees, which they have labeled "stick things" (*haiku uus*);
2. Cacti, which they call "stickers" (*hoi*);
3. Cultivated seasonals, which they designate as "things planted from seeds" (*haiku e es*);
4. Wild seasonals, to which they refer as being something "growing by itself" (*hejal vuus^{h}nim*).

The Papago leave wild perennials unlabeled as separate lexical items, given that they do not play significant roles in everyday life. They have other ways of referring to them, if the case should arise, but they have not been lexicalized as items of vocabulary. In other words, Papago vocabulary is *specialized* in this area of reference reflecting the particular reality that Papago people face in everyday life. Similar lexicalizing (word-creating) strategies are found in languages everywhere, which have developed specialized vocabularies to reflect the world they live in adaptively. However, because they are specialized, such vocabularies will dissipate if the conditions that they reflected change. In contemporary societies, for example, terms for new devices and media (*iPod, tablet, emoji, Facebook, SnapChat, Selfie*, etc.) have become specialized, mirroring new realities. As the technologies and related social realities change, they will disappear. Not long ago, a specialized vocabulary for referring to typewriters existed across languages. Today, most of the terms have virtually disappeared, for the simple reason that we no longer need them, unless of course someone is a collector of typewriters as antiques. A few terms within that specialized vocabulary have remained, however, because they have been transferred to describing the parts of a computer that are the same or similar, such as *keyboard* and *tab*.

> **VOCABULARY AND LEXICON**
>
> In linguistics, the term *vocabulary* refers to the actual lexemes (words and phrases) in a language, and *lexicon*, to the abstract knowledge of lexical structure. The lexicon is part of linguistic competence (*langue*) and vocabulary of communicative competence (*parole*). In practice, however, these two terms are often used interchangeably, unless there is a specific technical reason to use them differentially. A *specialized vocabulary* is a set of lexemes that refer to a specific subject or theme. It is sometimes called a *lexical field*.

A specialized vocabulary, such as that of the Papago, brings out how a language serves specific cultural needs and then doubles back on its speakers to guide their understanding of the sector of the world that it has encoded. Consider bodies of water. English has a sophisticated specialized vocabulary for classifying them—*lakes, oceans, rivers, streams, seas, creeks*, and so on. This vocabulary probably came into existence in English because of the historical importance of navigation and other water-based activities to English-speaking cultures. Needless to say, a similar specialized vocabulary is found in any culture that has faced similar historical conditions. People living in the desert, on the other hand, have fewer words for bodies of water, for obvious reasons. As another example, consider seating objects, which also reveal a sophisticated specialized vocabulary in English, including items such as those in Table 4.1:

TABLE 4.1 Specialized vocabulary related to seating: English

Object	*Distinguishing Features (among others)*
chair	seats one person, with a back
stool	seats one person, without a back
sofa	seats more than one person, with a back, soft
bench	seats more than one person, with a back, hard
lawn chair	seats one person, with a back that can be reclined

This type of vocabulary is also the result of the social importance ascribed to seating and sitting and is found wherever these activities are seen as important. On the contrary, in nomadic societies such as the Bedouins, the Mongols, and the Maasai, no parallel lexical specialization exists.

In sum, the cross-linguistic study of specialized vocabularies presents test cases for assessing relativity and codability features. An experiment by Peter Gordon (2004), for instance, examined counting terms used by the Pirahã people of Brazil. Because the language has three basic words— *one*, *two* and *many*—Gordon found that the Pirahã people have difficulty recalling or assessing tasks that require numbers higher than three. Given that they are hunter-gatherers a sophisticated specialized number vocabulary is not required by them to carry out their daily routines. Nevertheless, Gordon found that the Pirahã had developed non-lexicalizing strategies for referring to sophisticated numerical concepts if the need arose. Gordon's study has, actually, had significant implications for the universalist-versus-relativist debate on numeration and cognition. For neuroscientist Brian Butterworth (1999), numbers do not exist in the brain the way verbal symbols such as words do; they constitute a separate and unique kind of intelligence with its own brain module, located in the left parietal lobe. But this alone does not guarantee that the same type of counting ability will emerge homogeneously in all individuals. Rather, the reason a person falters at mathematics is not because of a "wrong gene" or faulty "engine part" in the left parietal lobe, but because the individual has not fully developed the number sense in the brain, and the reason for this is due to environmental and psychological factors. It is no coincidence, Butterworth maintains, that the left parietal lobe controls the movement of fingers, constituting a neurological clue to the evolution of our number sense, explaining why we count on our fingers. The non-linguistic nature of mathematics, according to Butterworth, may also explain why cultures that have very few symbols or words for numbers have still managed to develop counting strategies for practical purposes. This would explain the Pirahã strategies observed by Gordon, which has cast some light on the relation between number words and the perception of reality, an area that continues to be debated within mathematics and linguistics (Danesi 2019).

The research of French psychologist Jean Piaget (Piaget 1969; Piaget and Inhelder 1969) is of relevance to the foregoing discussion. In one of his experiments, Piaget presented a five-year-old child two matching sets of six eggs placed in six eggcups, asking him whether there were as many eggs as eggcups. The child replied affirmatively. Piaget then took the eggs out of the cups, bunching them together, with the egg-cups left where they were previously, asking the child whether or not all the eggs could be put into the cups, one in each cup and none left over. The answer he received this time was "no." So, when asked to count both eggs and cups, the child would correctly say that there were the same amounts. But, when asked if there were as many eggs as cups, the child did not reply correctly. The child, Piaget concluded, had not grasped the abstract properties of numeration, which are not affected by changes in the positions of objects. As Skemp (1971: 154) pointed out, Piaget's work has shown that counting is a learned skill that overlaps with verbal development: "counting is so much a part of the world around them that children learn to recite number-names not long after they learn to talk."

Kinship Terms

Two specialized vocabularies that have been of particular relevance to assessing the LRH are kinship and color terms. As mentioned at the start of this chapter, the specific kinship terms used in a language mirror how kin relations are perceived. The terms thus provide relevant insights for anthropologists into the cross-cultural structure of families and kinship relations. For instance, when comparing the traditional kinship systems of SAE-speaking cultures with, say, the Hawaiian kinship system among Malayo-Polynesian-speaking cultures, noticeable differences emerge (Haviland 2002). Like English, relations are distinguished by generation and by gender. But, in the Hawaiian system, relatives of the same generation and gender are named with the same term—for instance, the term used to refer to the *father* is used as well for the father's brother and the mother's brother (for which English uses *uncle*). Similarly, the mother, her sister, and the father's sister (for which English uses *aunt*) are classified together under a single term. Essentially, kinship reckoning in Hawaiian culture involves putting relatives of the same gender and generation into the same category. The Hawaiian system, called ambilineal, derives from the historical fact that child-rearing is shared by individuals affiliated to the father's or mother's kinship group.

Kinship systems were first discussed anthropologically by Lewis Henry Morgan in his 1871 work *Systems of Consanguinity and Affinity of the Human Family*. Morgan conducted ethnographical research on the Iroquois (a Native American people), finding that Iroquois society was matrilineal, from which he deduced that this mirrored the important role that motherhood played in that society. Work in anthropology has since shown that naming patterns reveal differing perceptions of kinship roles shaped by historical rearing practices and on the type of marriage relations that are assumed as basic. In his ethnography of the Nuer, a people of South Sudan and Ethiopia, Evans-Pritchard (1940) discovered that if a widow chooses to live with a lover outside of her deceased husband's kinship group, the lover is only considered to be the *genitor* (biological father) of any children the widow has with him, while her deceased husband continues to be considered the *pater* (legal father) of the children she had with him. As a result, the kin of the *pater* can take away his children whenever they choose. As Robin Fox (1977) suggests, the *pater-genitor* distinction is not uncommon, differentiating between the man who is socially recognized as assuming the father role and the man who is the biological father; similarly, the terms *mater* and *genitrix* are used to distinguish the female counterparts (see also Barnes 1961).

In a relevant study of kinship terms in the language of the Batak Toba (a people of North Sumatra, Indonesia), Nainggolan (2014) found that the word *amang*, which means "biological father," when doubled, *amang-amang*, means "husband." The same applies to motherhood, with *inang* meaning "biological mother," and *inang-inang* meaning "wife." In effect, the doubling of the same noun in this language, called an echo form, indicates that the *genitor* and *genitrix* concepts extend to marriage. In English, on the other hand, the two referents are distinguished lexically—*father* and *husband*, *mother* and *wife*—and, as such, can be autonomous, which is not the case in Batak Toba.

Abstract concepts, such as "fatherhood" and "motherhood," are rarely named in the same way across languages, because they are particularly high in social-emotional content (Bolinger 1968; Lévi-Strauss 1958). The term *lexical programming* (LP) can be used to refer to the ways in which lexical terms, such as those relating to kinship, have the ability to program the mind into seeing certain relations as being naturally "normal," even though they are actually culturally based. LP takes effect when lexical forms become part of habitual thought, as Whorf insightfully noted, and as will be discussed later in this chapter. To cite Boroditsky (2001: 12), "habits in language encourage habits in thought." Needless to say, changing the lexicon will change the habits of mind, as discussed above with the change in vocabulary from typewriters to computers. As Whorf emphasized, language does not close the mind, it simply shapes (or reshapes) it; but it also provides the resources for expanding it. To use an analogy with computer programming, human beings are both programmed by language and programmers of language.

Color Terms

Psychologists estimate that we can distinguish perhaps as many as 10 million hues (shades of color). This means that we would need an infinitude of terms to refer to each hue, which would be an impracticable task, linguistically and psychologically. So, a specific language steps in to make this practicable by classifying the color spectrum into a minimal set of lexical categories, as needed historically by a culture. This has a resulting lexical programming effect. If one were to place a finger at any point on the spectrum, there would be only a negligible difference in hue in the colors immediately adjacent to the finger at either side. Yet, a speaker of English describing the hues as the finger moves up and down the spectrum will do so with terms such as *purple, blue, green, yellow, orange,* and *red,* among others. This is because the English lexicon has pre-classified the content of the spectrum in specific ways, programming the mind of English speakers to see certain stretches of hue as belonging to a specific color category. There is nothing inherently "natural" about the English color scheme; it is a reflex of English vocabulary, not of Nature. What is a shade of color in one language, is a distinct color in another.

Specialized color vocabularies are, in effect, mental guides to color perception. Speakers of Shona, an indigenous African language, divide the color spectrum up into four main lexical categories from left to right—*cipswuka, citema, cicena,* and *cipswuka* (again); speakers of Bassa, a language of Liberia, segment it into two categories—*hui* and *ziza* (see Gleason 1955). When an English speaker refers to, say, a ball as *blue,* a Shona speaker may refer to it as either *cipswuka* or *citema,* and a Bassa speaker as *hui.* What a Shona speaker would consider as shades of *cicena,* an English speaker would see as two distinct colors, *green* and *yellow.* But such differences do not stop speakers of the different languages from relating their perceptual differences to each other. In all languages there exist verbal resources for referring to more specific gradations on the spectrum if the situation should require it. In English, the words *crimson, scarlet, vermilion,* for instance, make it possible to refer to types of *red.* But these are still felt by speakers to be subcategories of red, not distinct color categories on their own. Similar kinds of resources exist in Shona and Bassa.

A classic study of color terminology is that reported in 1953 by linguist Verne Ray. Ray interviewed the speakers of 60 different languages spoken in the south-western part of the USA. He showed them colored cards under uniform conditions of lighting, asking the speakers to name them in terms of their own words. Ray found that identifications according to language overlapped, contrasted, and coincided with each other. In Tenino and Chilcotin, for example, a part of the hue range of English *green* is covered by a term that includes *yellow.* In Wishram and Takelma, on the other hand, there are as many terms as in English, but the hue boundaries are different. In still other cases, there are more distinctions than in English. Ray concluded as follows (1953: 59): "Color systems serve to bring the world of color sensation into order so that perception may be relatively simple and behavioral response, particularly verbal response and communication, may be meaningful."

Ray's study, which appeared to support the WH in the area of color perception, contrasted somewhat with the findings of the Brown-Lenneberg study discussed in Chapter 3 (Brown and Lenneberg 1954; see also

Lenneberg and Roberts 1953), although codability factors were involved in a similar way. At the same time, Harold Conklin (1955) examined the color system of the Hanunóo of the Philippines. He found that there were four categories into which the Hanunóo grouped colors, in accordance with perceived patterns of light (the prefix *ma-* means "having" or "exhibiting"):

ma-biru ("darkness, blackness")
ma-lagti ("lightness, whiteness")
ma-rara ("redness, presence of red")
ma-latuy ("greenness, presence of green").

The *ma-biru* category implies absence of light, and thus includes not only English *black* but also many deep shades specified in English as *blue, violet, green, gray*, and so on. The *ma-lagti* category implies, instead, the presence of light, and thus includes English *white* and terms referring to lightly pigmented hues. The other two terms refer to hues that are connected to freshness and dryness in plants—*ma-rara* includes colors indicated in English by *red, orange,* and *yellow*, and *ma-latuy* referring instead to *green* and *brown* shades. The Hanunóo language can, of course, refer to color gradations more specifically than this, if the need should arise. But its basic system encodes a reality that is specific to the Hanunóo's environment and different from English and other SAE languages.

The question becomes: Do the color terms of a language affect what colors speakers actually see? And what connection does the physiology of perception play in color naming? Whorf (1956) addressed these succinctly as follows:

> For instance, if a race of people had the physiological defect of being able to see only the color blue, they would hardly be able to formulate the rule that they saw only blue. The term blue would convey no meaning to them, their language would lack color terms, and their words denoting their various sensations of blue would answer to, and translate, our words light, dark, white, black, and so on, not our word blue. In order to formulate the rule or norm of seeing only blue, they would need exceptional moments in which they saw other colors.

Is Whorf correct? Do specialized color terms program the mind to see external color physically in specific ways? American anthropologists Brent Berlin and Paul Kay (1969) decided to study these questions head-on. Their study became a key one in the debate on the LRH, since it seemed to show definitively that differences in color terms are only superficial matters that conceal universal principles of color perception. Berlin and Kay asked native speakers of a host of different languages to sort over 300 color chips into verbal categories that could not be subsumed within any other category. The instructions to subjects included the following:

1. The term must be a single lexeme (for example, *brown*, but not *yellow-brown* or *brown-yellow*).
2. Morphemic variants are eliminated (for example, *brownish*)
3. The meaning cannot be covered by any other color term (for example, *crimson* as a type of *red*).
4. The term cannot be limited to a narrow semantic field (for example, *blonde* is restricted to referents such as *hair*, *wood*, and *beer*).
5. The term must be salient (for example, *the color of his suit* is not salient for all speakers).
6. Color terms that are names of an object are excluded (for example, *gold* and *silver*).
7. Foreign words are excluded.

On the basis of the judgments of the native speakers, Berlin and Kay came to the conclusion that there were "focal points" in basic (single-term) color vocabularies, which clustered in certain predictable ways. They identified eleven focal points, corresponding to the English words *black*, *white*, *red*, *yellow*, *green*, *blue*, *brown*, *purple*, *pink*, *orange*, and *gray*. Not all the languages they investigated had separate terms for each of these colors, but there emerged a pattern that suggested to Berlin and Kay that there was a fixed sequence of color-naming across cultures:

- If a language had two colors, then the names were equivalents of English *black* and *white*.
- If it had three color terms, then the third one corresponded to *red*.
- A four-term system had a term for either *yellow* or *green*, but not both.
- A five-term system had terms for both *yellow* and *green*.
- A six-term system included a term for *blue*.
- A seven-term system had a term for *brown*.
- Finally, terms for *purple*, *pink*, *orange*, and *gray* were found to occur in any combination in languages that had the previous focal terms.

Berlin and Kay found that languages with, say, a four-term system consisting of *black*, *white*, *red*, and *brown* did not exist. Each of the languages lexicalized virtually identical hues for each color category, corresponding roughly to the same shade in the Munsell color system, a system developed in the early 1900s by Albert H. Munsell, an American portrait painter. The Munsell color system is still used by manufacturers of such products as foods, paints, paper, plastics, and textiles who must often name colors precisely. By way of conclusion, Berlin and Kay posited that the naming of

TABLE 4.2 The universal properties of perception related to color

	Terms (English Equivalents)	Examples of Languages
2	white, black	Jale (New Guinea), Ngombe (Africa)
3	white, black, red	Arawak (Caribbean), Swahili (Eastern Africa)
4	white, black, red, yellow/green	Ibo (Nigeria), Tongan (Polynesia)
5	white, black, red, yellow, green	Tarascan (Mexico), !Kung (Southern Africa)
6	white, black, red, yellow, green, blue	Tamil (India, Sri Lanka), Mandarin (China)
7	white, black, red, yellow, green, blue, brown	Nez Percé (Montana), Javanese
8	white, black, red, yellow, green, blue, brown (purple, pink, orange, gray)	English, Zuñi (New Mexico), Dinka (Sudan), Tagalog (Philippines)

Note: Adapted from Berlin and Kay (1969).

color is based on universal properties of perception, not on any relativity effects. Examples of languages possessing from two to 11 focal terms are given in Table 4.2.

Paul Kay revised the sequence in 1975 in order to account for the fact that certain languages, such as Japanese, encode a color category that does not exist in English, and that can only be rendered in English as *green-blue*. This category, which Kay labeled *grue*, may occur before or after *yellow* in the original sequence. Then, Kay and Luisa Maffi (1999) responded to data collected by Stephen Levinson (2000) on the Yélî language of Papua New Guinea. Levinson had found that there are sectors on the color spectrum for which Yélî has no names that would be subsumed under the focal color categories of the Berlin-Kay model, pointing out that Yélî is "a language where a semantic field of color has not yet jelled," and thus does not fit in with the universal evolution of color categories (Levinson 2000: 54). Kay and Maffi countered that, however, such a referential domain can emerge over time, dubbing this an Emergence Hypothesis, which has never been confirmed in any empirical way since.

It has also been found that the Berlin-Kay sequence does not reflect the lexicons of languages that they themselves studied. For example, Italian and Russian do not have one color term for *blue* but, rather, distinguish *light blue* and *dark blue* as distinct focal colors— respectively, *celeste* and *azzurro* in Italian, and *goluboy* and *siniy* in Russian. As Winawer, Witthoft, Frank, Wu, Wade, and Boroditsky (2007) found, this lexical difference has relativity effects on color perception. In one experiment, the researchers found that Russian speakers performed more quickly on a matching task when the *blue* hues belonged to different linguistic categories, whereas

English subjects were much slower, since the color stimuli were perceived as belonging to the same category.

Despite such counterexamples and counterarguments, the Berlin-Kay study has remained a reference point in any assessment of the LRH, guiding subsequent research on color perception. Eleanor Rosch (1975), for instance, examined color terminology among the Dani people of West Irian, who have a two-color system similar to the Bassa one. Using a recognition-memory experiment, Rosch found that the Dani recognized focal colors better than non-focal ones. She also found that they learned color terms more easily when they were paired with focal points. Such findings suggested to Rosch that languages provided a guide to the interpretation of color, but they did not affect its perception in any way. A year later, Bornstein, Kessen and Weiskopf (1976) presented infants aged four months light stimuli of different frequencies corresponding to different color hues. The pattern of responses indicated to the researchers that the children distinguished between the focal colors, but not between successive hues (that is, different hues of *red* are all *red*); in effect, the researchers claimed that the infants responded to different hues of color in terms of focality, suggesting the presence of a universal color perception at an age younger than previously expected and thus existing before the acquisition of culture-specific color terms. From such work, support for the Berlin-Kay model is still strong today. David Ludden (2015), for instance, has remarked that their study made it obvious that:

> Although the colors of the visible light spectrum vary along a continuum, our visual system is maximally sensitive to four specific regions—red, green, yellow, and blue—which we then perceive as the four focal colors. Languages around the world tend to organize their color systems around these four focal colors. That is, languages will have names for these four colors before they'll have basic terms for colors like orange or purple. This four-color distinction is an important element of Westernized global color schemes, as for example in the four suits of an Uno deck or in the logos for Microsoft and Google.

But a problem remains that, ironically, reflects linguistic relativity indirectly—namely, the focal colors posited by Berlin and Kay, and subsequent corroborating researchers, corresponded to the color terms of English, and this may have been an unconscious Whorfian factor itself in shaping how the different experiments produced their particular results. It is also relevant to note that the Berlin-Kay focal color system has roots in Sir Isaac Newton's system of primary colors (Newton 1704: 114–117) that coincide more or less with Berlin and Kay's focal colors (see Figure 4.1).

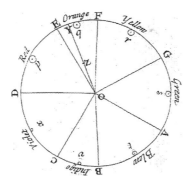

FIGURE 4.1 Newton's Color Wheel

The colors are arranged clockwise in the order they are perceived to occur on the rainbow, with each spoke of the wheel assigned a letter corresponding to the notes of the Dorian musical scale. The notion of focal color can probably be traced back to this early classification and seen as a "natural" way to understand color. But, as Marc Bornstein (2006) remarks: "the physics of color, the psychophysics of color discrimination, and the psychology of color naming are not isomorphic" (see also Cibelli, Xu, Austerweil, Griffiths, and Regier 2016; Pitchford and Mullen 2006). Also, one can never ignore the use of metaphor in color naming. Swahili has three focal terms, but its color vocabulary is enlarged by figurative reference to objects (for example, yellow = *manjano* "turmeric") and through borrowing from other languages (blue = *buluu*). As anthropologist Roger Wescott (1980) has shown, metaphor may even be the source of the color names themselves. In Hittite, for instance, words for colors initially designated plant and tree names, such as *poplar, elm, cherry, oak*, and so on.

Barbara Saunders (Saunders 1995; Saunders and Brakel 1997) has also argued that the Berlin-Kay model contains the assumption of English terms as the focal colors. John Lucy (1997b) pointed out deficiencies in the Berlin-Kay study, such as a lack of consideration of the meanings of color terms across languages and their grammatical distribution (how the term is used). He refers to the Conklin study of Hanunóo mentioned above as a demonstration of what a study may reveal about a language's color naming system without any biases—biases summarized insightfully by Wierzbicka (2006) as follows:

1. There is a tendency to find some explanation for languages that lack a word for a focal color, even if it is not plausible.
2. There is a lack of consideration of the semantic range of any given assumed color naming in a language.

3. The Western universalist tradition "imposes on other languages and cultures one's own conceptual grid" and does not reflect "the native's point of view."

As Regier, Kay, Gilbert, and Ivry (2010) have also pointed out, supporting Wierzbicka's critique, the universalist perspective goes back to the nineteenth century:

> In the mid-nineteenth century, various scholars, notably William Gladstone (1858) and Lazarus Geiger (1880), noted that the speakers of ancient written languages did not name colors as precisely and consistently—as they saw it—as the speakers of modern European languages. They proposed a universal evolutionary sequence in which color vocabulary evolves in tandem with an assumed biological evolution of the color sense.

As the foregoing discussion suggests, there really is no way to prove one or the other perspective vis-à-vis the LRH—universalist or relativist—as exclusionary models. As Paul Kay himself, with Terry Regier, pointed out in a 2006 overview of the color debate: "There are universal constraints on color naming, but at the same time, differences in color naming across languages cause differences in color cognition and/or perception."

Grammar

As Whorf emphasized, relativity effects are not limited to the lexicon, but are found at all levels of language from the phonological to the grammatical (Chapter 3). With regard to the latter, Whorf (1940: 230) explained the traditional view as follows:

> Languages have grammars, which are assumed to be merely norms of conventional and social correctness, but the use of language is supposed to be guided not so much by them as by correct, rational, or intelligent thinking. Thought, in this view, does not depend on grammar but on laws of logic or reason which are supposed to be the same for all observers of the universe—to represent a rationale in the universe that can be "found" independently by all intelligent observers, whether they speak Chinese or Choctaw. In our own culture, the formulations of mathematics and of formal logic have acquired the reputation of dealing with this order of things: that is, with the realm and laws of pure thought. Natural logic holds that different languages are essentially parallel methods for expressing this one-and-the-same rationale of thought and, hence, differ really in but minor ways which may seem important only because they are seen at close range.

Vocabulary and Grammar   71

TABLE 4.3 Example of verbal concepts as related to spatial experiences

English Concept	Navajo Concept Translated Literally
one dresses	one moves into clothing
one lives	one moves about here and there
one is young	one moves about newly
to sing	to move words out of an enclosed space
to greet someone	to move a round solid object to meet someone

Cross-linguistic grammatical analysis is again one of the main ways in which the LRH can be put to the test. Consider the verb system of Navajo (Faltz 1998). In that language, verbs are marked for designating specific aspects of motion and of objects affected by motion. This entails a predisposition to seeing verbal concepts as related to spatial experiences, again conforming to the physical concept of spacetime in physics and the Hopi language. This perspectival aspect of Navajo grammar stands in contrast to English grammar, as shown in Table 4.3.

Using an analogous term to lexical programming (LP), the term *grammatical programming* (GP) can be employed to describe the differences in mental perspective entailed by grammatical differences, such as those in Table 4.3. GP implies that specific grammatical categories condition how speakers view aspects of reality, or at least to attend to them as necessary. Recall from Chapter 2 Langacker's (1987, 1990) analysis of nouns as eliciting images of referents that trace a region in mind-space—for example, a count noun is imagined as referring to something that enfolds a bounded region, whereas a mass noun is visualized as designating a non-bounded region. The noun *water* elicits an image of a non-bounded region (unless it is part of a body of water), whereas the noun *rock* evokes an image of a bounded region. This conceptual dichotomy has specific grammatical effects—*rocks* can be counted, *water* cannot; *rock* has a plural form, *water* does not (unless the referential domain is metaphorical); *rock* can be preceded by an indefinite article (*a rock*), *water* cannot; and so on. Grammar is, Langacker asserts, a strategy for organizing our perception of things in the world as they stand in relation to one another.

Consider the relation between the active and passive: *Sarah ate the apple* versus *The apple was eaten by Sarah*. The active sentence presents a specific perspectival scenario—the subject (*Sarah*) is in the foreground and the object (*apple*) in the background. As a consequence, the image of the eater is larger than that of the object being eaten in mind space. A change from active to passive entails a shift in this perspectival scene. The passive sentence brings the *apple* to the foreground, relegating the eater, *Sarah*, to the background. The action of *eating* is now spotlighted on the object, which is larger as an image than *Sarah*, who recedes to the background. In effect, each type of sentence encodes a different mental angle from which an action can be seen.

The relation of mental perspective to grammar has been described by Langacker (1988: 7) as follows:

> A pivotal claim of cognitive grammar is that linguistic expressions and grammatical constructions embody conventional imagery, which constitutes an essential aspect of their semantic value. In choosing a particular expression or construction, a speaker construes the conceived situation in a certain way, i.e. he selects one particular image (from a range of alternatives) to structure its conceptual content for expressive purposes.

Mental perspective is shaped by all kinds of GP, as Langacker suggests. As another example, consider the use of the English prepositions *since* and *for* in sentences such as the following:

1. I have been living here *since* 2020.
2. I have known Jennie *since* November.
3. I have not been able to sleep *since* Monday.
4. I have been living here *for* ten years.
5. I have known Jennie *for* nine months.
6. I have not been able to sleep *for* seven days.

The complements that follow *since* are imagined as points on a timeline (consecutive years, days, months, etc.): *2020, Monday, November*. Complements that follow *for*, on the other hand, reflect an image of time as a measurable quantity: *ten years, nine months, seven days*. Now, in Italian, only the timeline concept is involved, borne out by the exclusive use of the preposition *da* ("from") to cover the same two grammatical categories of English. The corresponding sentences in Italian would be the following:

1. Vivo qui *dal* 2020.
2. Conosco Jennie *da* novembre.
3. Non dormo *da* lunedì.
4. Vivo qui *da* dieci anni.
5. Conosco Jennie *da* nove mesi.
6. Non riesco a dormire *da* sette giorni.

The difference in this sector of grammar is thus tied to a difference in the perception of time in imagistic terms. The two are inextricable, as we shall see in Chapter 6.

TABLE 4.4 Examples American Indian Grammatical Categories

Language	"He will give it to you"	Structure in English
Wishram	a-â-i-m-l-úd-a	will-he-him-you-to-give-will
Takelma	ök-t-xpi-nk	will-give-to-you-he or they
South Paiute	maya-vaania-aka-ana-mi	give-will-visible thing-visible creature-you
Yana	ba-ja-ma-si-wa-numa	round thing-away-to-does-unto-you
Nootka	o-yi-aqλ-at-eik	that-give-will-done unto-you are
Navaho	n-a-yi-diho-a	you-to transitive-will-round thing

Source: Sapir and Swadesh (1946).

Rudolf Arnheim (1969: 239–242) presents a similar argument—conjunctions and prepositions are hardly just formal devices of grammar; they provide insights into how thought unfolds in terms of mental perspective:

> I referred in an earlier chapter to the barrier character of "but," quite different from "although," which does not stop the flow of action but merely burdens it with a complication. Causal relations…are directly perceivable actions; therefore "because" introduces an effectuating agent, which pushes things along. How different is the victorious overcoming of a hurdle conjured up by "in spite of" from the displacement in "either-or" or "instead;" and how different is the stable attachment of "with" or "of" from the belligerent "against."

A cross-linguistic study by Sapir, reported in Sapir and Swadesh (1946), is another case in point. Sapir asked (bilingual) speakers of several Native languages of the south-western United States to render the English sentence *He will give it to you* in their respective languages (see Table 4.4).

As this shows, syntax is the mechanism that shapes how events in the world are related to each other, not as dependent on universal rules of combination. The particular syntactic pattern in a language reveals how the "stream of consciousness" in sentences is structured. This term was introduced by Alexander Bain in 1855 in his book *The Senses and the Intellect*, but it was William James (1890) who introduced it into psychology, to describe the flow of personal thoughts that occurs below the threshold of consciousness and mirrored in the syntax of sentences.

Habitual Thought

Whorf saw habitual thought as indistinguishable from language. He put it as follows (Whorf 1941: 81):

> By "habitual thought" and "thought world" I mean more than simply language, i.e. than the linguistic patterns themselves. I include all the

analogical and suggestive value of the patterns (e.g., our "imaginary space" and its distant implications), and all the give-and-take between language and the culture as a whole, wherein is a vast amount that is not linguistic but yet shows the shaping influence of language. In brief, this "thought world" is the microcosm that each man carries about within himself, by which be measures and understands what he can of the macrocosm.

Although it goes back to Aristotle, the modern-day concept of *habit* is commonly associated with behaviorism, a school of psychology which first studied the formation of habits of mind empirically. The key notion in this framework is that of the *conditioned response*, which was, as is well-known, developed initially by the Russian Ivan Pavlov in 1902, on the basis of his research with dogs. Pavlov's original experiment is worth summarizing here for the sake of argument. He presented a piece of meat to a hungry dog, producing the expected spontaneous response of salivation in the dog. Pavlov called this reaction the dog's *unconditioned response*, because it is part of instinctual behavior. Then he rang a bell at the same time as he presented the meat stimulus a number of times, discovering that the dog eventually salivated only to the ringing of the bell, without the presence of meat. Clearly, the bell ringing, which would not have triggered the salivation instinctively, had brought about a conditioned response in the dog. Over time, this conditioned reaction became part of the dog's habitual pattern of responses. In 1903, right after Pavlov's groundbreaking experiments, B. R. Andrews, writing in in the *American Journal of Psychology*, defined a habit as "a more or less fixed way of thinking, willing, or feeling acquired through previous repetition of a mental experience." Shortly thereafter, habit-formation became a major theme in behaviorist psychology (Watson 1913; Skinner 1938).

Today, behaviorism is no longer dominant as a psychological school, but it continues to be effective in specific pedagogical and clinical practices. The emergence of cognitivism as mainstrem in the 1960s coincided with the rise of Chomskyan theory in linguistics, moving away from conditioning theories and theories of habit-formation. The term *habituation* is now used as a replacement for the term *conditioning* (Bouton 2007).

There is little doubt that Whorf was affected by theories of habit-formation during his times, as were other prominent linguists, such as Leonard Bloomfield (1933). However, not all these were based on conditioning experiences. For example, psychologist Edward Tolman (1932) connected habits with cognition and the Gestalt psychologists (Koffka 1921; Köhler 1925; Wertheimer 1923) emphasized the study of mental habits as deriving from experience as a unified whole, not as the result of conditioning responses from isolated stimuli. It is the Tolman-Gestalt view that is inherent in Whorf's idea of "thought world."

It is not clear whether Whorf came across the writings of pragmatist philosopher and semiotician Charles Peirce (1931–1958), but Whorf's views of habitual thought also overlapped with Peirce's idea of "habituescence," which itself harken back to the ideas of Alexander Bain (1868). Habituescence is Peirce's term for how our semiotic systems predispose us to view the world in terms of the habits they condition (Whorf 1940: 229). In effect, as Peirce and Whorf would have it, habits of language are habits of mind.

Epilogue

As discussed in this chapter, the cross-linguistic study of specialized vocabularies and grammatical categories provides a means for examining the LRH in concrete ways. Differences in lexical and grammatical programming are often the sources of the malapropisms that result from translation. Charlie Crocker (2007, 2015) provides examples of these, having collected English-language signs in non-English countries. An example is a sign he found inside the lobby of a hotel in Paris, written in English: *Please leave your values at the front desk* (Crocker 2007: 5). To native speakers of English, this sign will likely be interpreted as either hilarious or perplexing—How can you leave your *values* anywhere? The problem is to be located in the lexical domains of the two languages.

This example highlights a common and persistent problem manifested by second language learners as well—like the translator of the hotel sign, they put together expressions or messages with the new foreign words and phrases that reflect the concepts they bear in their native language. In other words, they are conveying their native thought habits through the new structures. In the example above, the English word *value* was assumed by the French translator to coincide in meaning and use with the French word *valeur*. One of the meanings of *valeur*, and the one obviously intended by the translator, is rendered by *valuables*, not *values*, in English. So, the translator simply assumed that *valeur* meant the same as *value* and thus used it with this meaning when creating the hotel sign. The result was an English sentence with a word in it that reflects French, not English, meaning. When overlaps in meaning occur, the translation is accurate; when they do not, it is anomalous (Danesi 2017a).

Although Whorf did not deal with bilingualism directly, his ideas clearly have implications for its study. For example, an area in which to test the LRH is in the habit that bilinguals display of switching between their two codes as they communicate. This allows them to do several things, including filling in conceptual gaps in one language from the other. Bilinguals have access to two language systems and so, when a conceptual-referential gap occurs in one, they can easily fill it with an item from their other system (if it exists) as they speak. For example, an Italian-English bilingual may use the word *simpatico* in a sentence such as "I think he is *simpatico*," because the Italian term covers a broader range of meanings than do English equivalents such as *nice, charming,* and *sweet*. There are other reasons to switch codes, of course, including to show allegiance to a group, seeing certain topics as being more appropriately expressed in one code rather than another, and so on. But, often, it is simply that the two languages allow the bilingual speaker to move between two thought worlds and find the linguistic resources in one or the other to fill conceptual gaps. This is clearly related to the LRH: Do the vocabularies and grammars of the two languages guide the bilingual's thoughts? It would be a striking finding indeed if evidence emerged to answer this question in the positive, for it would be concrete evidence in support of the LRH.

Lexical gaps occur constantly; those filled by one language are left void by another. Nonetheless, as Whorf knew, these can always be filled with approximations and paraphrases. Below are lexical encodings of concepts that are missing in English as illustrative cases in point:

- Ulwa (a language of Nicaragua) uses *alag* to indicate "the fold of skin under the chin."
- Tulu (a language of India) has *karelu* to refer to "the mark left on the skin by wearing something tight."
- German has the word *Kummerspeck*, literally "grief bacon," to designate "the excess weight gained from overeating caused by emotional problems."
- Wagiman (a language of Australia) uses the verb *murrma* to refer to "walking along the water searching for something with one's feet."
- Spanish has the reflexive verb *achaplinarse* to indicate "hesitating and then running away in the manner of Charlie Chaplin."
- Farsi has the word *mahj* to designate "looking beautiful after a disease;" and *nakhur* for "a camel that will not give milk until its nostrils have been tickled."
- Czech has the word *nedovtipa* to refer to "someone who finds it difficult to take a hint."
- Pacuense (spoken on Eastern Island) has the word *tingo* for "borrowing things from a friend's house, one by one, until there's nothing left."

If these concepts should be ever needed, speakers of English (or other languages) could either borrow the relevant words, devise paraphrases, or create native lexemes for them. As Whorf maintained, it would be foolhardy to pretend that we all think exactly the same, even though we can easily understand each other.

Discussion Questions and Activities

Chapter Questions

1. Among cultures, do differences in vocabulary and grammar entail differences in cultural organization and thus of understanding?
2. What can we learn about linguistic relativity from studying kinship and color terms?
3. Are habits of mind equivalent to habits of language?

Related Questions

4. What aspects of the Berlin-Kay study are relevant to the universalist-versus-relativist debate in linguistics? Which counterarguments can be given?
5. Do you think that habitual thought equals language (its vocabulary, its grammar, etc.), as Whorf claimed? If so, why so? If not, why not?
6. How many names do you know for different breeds of dogs? Give the social meaning that each one elicits. Then translate these into any other language you know and compare each one.
7. Do you think that syntax reflects the stream of consciousness? Do you know any examples of such thinking from literature?
8. If you know another language, how does its grammar refer to motion? Is it different from English verbs?

Activities

1. If you know another language, give the equivalents in that language of the following English terms. Point out any differences that may emerge in terms of the LRH.
    (a) mother
    (b) father
    (c) son
    (d) daughter
    (e) brother
    (f) sister
    (g) grandfather
    (h) grandmother
    (i) uncle
    (j) aunt
    (k) male cousin
    (l) female cousin.

78 Vocabulary and Grammar

2. Similarly, if you know another language, give the equivalents in that language of the following English terms referring to plants. Point out any differences that may emerge in terms of the LRH.
   (a) rose
   (b) tree
   (c) weed
   (d) shrub
   (e) dandelion.
3. Now, do the same exercise for the following color terms.
   (a) red
   (b) green
   (c) yellow
   (d) blue
   (e) pink.
4. Make a list of the emotion(s) designated by color terms in English, giving a probable reason why the terms and the emotions were linked in the first place. For example: *green = envy* ("You're green with envy"). Green is the color of grass and used in an associated English proverb, *The grass is greener on the other side*, and thus may indicate that one envies what someone else has. Also, if you know another language compare its emotional meanings associated with color terms to those in English.
   (a) blue
   (b) yellow
   (c) brown
   (d) gray
   (e) red.
5. Passive sentences are often cited as being grammatical transformations of active ones. However, there is a difference in perspectival meaning between them, as discussed in this chapter. Indicate what this difference is in the given active and passive pairs below.
   (a) He ate the apple.
       The apple was eaten by him.
   (b) They closed the store early.
       The store was closed early.
   (c) Alex received a high grade on the test.
       A high grade was received by Alex on the test.
   (d) Someone wrote that play in the medieval ages.
       That play was written in the medieval ages.

5
DISCOURSE AND TRANSLATION

Prologue

As discussed in previous chapters, cross-linguistic analysis has been a primary method for testing, assessing, and debating the LRH. Where linguistic categories are different, the differences are examined to determine whether they may produce relativity effects or not, and these can then be further studied in terms of codability on the Whorfian Scale, from greater to less. Consider, for example, how speakers of English and speakers of Navajo (Faltz 1998) express intentions of *going* and *running*:

> *English:* I have to go there.
> *Navajo:* It is only good that I shall go there (*paraphrase*).
> *English:* I will have to make the horse run.
> *Navajo:* The horse is running for me (*paraphrase*).

A schematic analysis of the two ways of encoding the same verbal referents reveals that the role of speaker (the *ego*) in controlling a situation is seen differentially—namely, by the *ego* (English), versus through the *ego* (Navajo). The two English utterances suggest, in effect, that English discursive style projects the *ego*, as represented by the pronoun *I*, into the foreground of a motion scene, indicating that the actor in a situation is in control of the situation. In contrast, the Navajo utterances project the *ego* into the background, with the actions themselves and the other players involved in them projected into the foreground, implying that a situation is not directly controlled by the *ego* but, rather, that it unfolds through the *ego*. The question becomes: Do examples such as these imply that differences in how speakers talk about something in particular is guided by a broader form of linguistic relativity, called *discursive relativity*, shaping how they envision themselves as actors in the world? In other words: Do differences in *discourse*—how speakers talk about something—reflect differences in the perception of how *actors* in a situation are expected to *act*?

This chapter looks at how discourse practices and styles can be used to examine the LRH at a pragmatic level. It also considers translation as a primary technique in examining cross-linguistic differences, from lexical to pragmatic ones—including relevant work in the field of Machine Translation.

The questions guiding the discussion in this chapter are the following:

1. Do discourse practices produce relativity effects? Do they guide social behaviors?
2. What does translation reveal about linguistic relativity?
3. What can we learn from studying Machine Translation vis-à-vis linguistic relativity?

Discursive Relativity

Discourse is a broad term referring to patterns of expression and meaning-negotiation in spoken or written communication; it is part of a system of linguistically-based interaction principles that guide conversations and dialogues. As mentioned previously, Leo Spitzer's *Stilstudien* (1928) was an early treatise on how discourse styles guide social habits and activities. The way people talk about a situation reveals how they are predisposed to perceive their role, and that of others, in that situation—as we saw above with the English-versus-Navajo examples. By talking about the world in a certain way, we come to perceive it as somehow the truth of the matter, becoming habitual thought, to use Whorf's term from the previous chapter (see Keller 2011).

The study of the relation between discourse and thought goes back to antiquity. Socrates and Plato introduced the concept of *dialogue* as a distinctive form of philosophical inquiry; the Sumerian disputations were also written in the form of dialogues; and so on. It was Russian semiotician Mikhail Bakhtin who was the first to examine discourse in relativity terms, that is, as revealing how people project themselves into social situations as revealed in how they talk (Bakhtin 1981). Understanding one's role in the world is thus shaped through dialogic structures. So, too, is one's reaction to situations. Conversations can be framed to be aggressive or subdued, competitive or cooperative, depending on situation. In the case of competitive speech, the language used involves the use of lexical and stylistic devices that will be perceived as adversarial, whereas, in the case of cooperative speech, the devices chosen are designed to convey that the speakers share similar meanings. For instance, it is marked by features such as the following:

1. Speakers build upon each other's comments with consensus expressions ("That's true," "I agree").
2. They use hedges strategically to indicate consent ("Uh-huh," "Yeah," "Sure," "Right").
3. When disagreement surfaces, it is negotiated with various other hedges ("Yeah, but, maybe").
4. Tag questions are used to ensure consent ("You agree, don't you?").

This unconscious discourse script imparts a sense of togetherness among speakers. As Robin Lakoff (1975) has observed, speakers regularly refrain from saying what they mean in many situations in the service of the higher goal of cooperation in its broadest sense—that is, to fulfill one of the primary social functions of amicable conversation.

Conflictual conversations are marked by devices that stand in direct contrast to the ones given above:

1. Interlocutors tend to contradict one another's comments ("That's really not true," "I wouldn't say that").
2. They use hedges to indicate dissent ("No-no," "No way," "Not true").
3. Difference of opinion is indicated as well with various other hedges ("Sure, but, maybe").
4. Tag questions are used to challenge an interlocutor ("You don't mean that, do you?").

Discourse is not, clearly, a vehicle for the simple exchange of information. As Bakhtin (1986: 68) put it: "a passive understanding of the meaning of perceived speech is only an abstract aspect of the actual whole of actively responsive understanding." This is why the interlocutor is constantly in a reactive state from the first word to the unfolding treatment of a topic in a repartee. As Bakhtin and Voloshinov (1986: 102) explain:

> For each word of the utterance that we are in the process of understanding, we, as it were, lay down a set of our own answering words. The greater their number and weight, the deeper and more substantial our understanding will be. Any true understanding is dialogic in nature. Understanding is to utterance as one line of dialogue is to the next.

The Bakhtinian perspective implies that even formulaic speech involves inter-subjective understanding. Consider so-called *phatic communion*, which was first studied by the anthropologist Bronislaw Malinowski (1922), who coined the term to characterize verbal contact protocols and ritualistic talk, as manifestations of habitual thought (see Goffman 1959). A simple greeting protocol such as "Hi, how are you?", is an example of a formulaic phatic ritual enacted between individuals who know each other. The words in this case do not bear literal meaning referring to the state of health of the interlocutor—they are constituents in a speech ritual intended to acknowledge that the interlocutors know each other. Indeed, an expected answer, such as "Not bad, and you?", has nothing to do with the health of the speaker; it is the expected response in the contact ritual. But when a physician uses the exact same speech formula, it is hardly perceived as a phatic protocol; rather, it is understood as a literal query about the patient's health. The social situation is thus critical in determining how phatic speech is to be interpreted. As Finkbeiner, Meibauer, and Schumacher (2012) have shown, discourse contexts induce a reaction in the brain that guides the interpretive paths that interlocutors take in the discourse sequence.

The term *bricolage* was used by anthropologist Claude Lévi-Strauss in his 1962 book *La pensée sauvage* to describe ritualistic discourses. To outsiders, a certain discourse ritual may appear to be meaningless but, to insiders, it is part of a coherent unity of meaning embedded in the verbal devices chosen. All societies, Lévi-Strauss claimed, create solutions to their dilemmas by using the linguistic resources that they have in a collective (*bricolage*) fashion. Discourse suggests that cognition is a bricolage habit of thought, shared by speakers in the act of speaking (Hymes 1961, 1966; Hutchins 1995). The notion of *discursive relativity*, developed by such researchers as John Lucy (1996), Dan Slobin (1996), and John Haviland (1996), was necessitated in part to account for this phenomenon. Lucy (1996: 52) defined the study of discursive relativity as follows:

> Any investigation of the relation between language and thought must also cope with the question [of] whether patterns of use have an impact on thought either directly or by amplifying or channeling any effects due to linguistic structure. We can call this the hypothesis of discursive relativity, a relativity stemming from diversity in the functional (or goal-oriented) configuration of language means in the course of (inter)action.

Penelope Brown and Stephen Levinson (1987) have documented how politeness phatic protocols involve discursive relativity. They identified three variables that guide the choice of politeness strategies in specific situations: (1) the social distance of the interlocutors, (2) the relative power of one interlocutor over the other, and (3) the absolute ranking of impositions between interlocutors as prescribed by cultural interaction practices.

In East Asian cultures, politeness is oriented towards acknowledging the positions or roles of all the participants, as well as adherence to formality norms appropriate to the situation. Japanese has two main politeness protocols: one for intimate acquaintances, such as family members and friends, and one for other people, each of which is marked by morphological subsystems—some verbs, nouns, and pronouns, for example, are used to reference the gender, age, rank, and degree of acquaintance of the interlocutors. In effect, politeness protocols reflect and define culture-specific views of human relations. As Jack Sidnell (2019: 467) aptly remarks, "Human social relations, for instance, are constituted in large part through the use of language."

Lucy (1997a) has identified three main strands in the study of relativity, encompassing linguistic and discursive relativity:

1. *Structure-centered:* This refers to research that focuses on structural peculiarities in a language and their possible implications for shaping thought.
2. *Domain-centered:* This refers to research that chooses a specific semantic domain (for instance, color, space, etc.) and then compares it across linguistic and cultural groups. Speakers rely on the linguistic conceptualization of color, space, motion, and so on in performing ordinary tasks.
3. *Behavior-centered:* This refers to research that compares behaviors of different linguistic groups, searching for the causes in the respective linguistic systems (as, for example, verb usage differences).

Work on discursive relativity would fall into the third type of approach. For example, the use of gendered titles would fall under this rubric. In English, the titles *Mrs.*, *Miss*, *Ms.* and *Mr.* are hardly formulaic conveyors of the biological genders of the interlocutors in a situation; rather, they imply social relativity patterns. The female titles, *Mrs.* and *Miss*, encode the status of a female interlocutor as being married or not. The male title, *Mr.*, bears no such information (King 1991). This pattern is broken by the title *Ms.*, which was introduced in the 1970s to provide a socially-neutral title parallel to *Mr.*, eliminating marital status from the semantics of female titles.

Indirect reference to gender through lexemic or morphemic structures shapes perception of people and events in a situation. In English, the word for "general human being" is, traditionally, *man*, which coincides semantically with "the male person." The word actually meant "person" or "human being" in Old English and was equally applicable to both genders (Miller and Swift 1971, 1988). Old English did have separate words to distinguish the gender of speakers—*wer* for "adult male" and *wif* for "adult female." The composite forms *waepman* and *wifman* meant "adult male person" and "adult female person," respectively. In time, *wifman* evolved into the modern word *woman* and *wif* narrowed its meaning to *wife*. The word *man* then replaced *wer* and *waepman* as a specific term distinguishing an adult male from an adult female, but it continued to be used in generalizations referring to human beings. The result of merging these semantic domains rendered females socially invisible. Studies investigating the meanings that are elicited when *man* is used as a generic reference have confirmed this (Doyle 1985). Changes made to the English language over recent decades have attempted to correct this perception. But marked perceptions still exist, being more subtle, constituting suggestive evidence of discursive relativity effects.

Gender categories in language guide discursive practices. For example, in Koasati (an indigenous language spoken in Louisiana), men say *lawawhol* to refer to "lifting," while women say *lakawhos* (Haas 1944; Kimball 1991). Arguably, the Koasati people perceive the lifting abilities of the two genders as different and thus see the need to convey this dissimilarity routinely through morphological differentiation. In the language spoken on the Island of Carib in the West Indies, women use the word *kachi* for "sun" while the men use *hueyu* (Taylor 1977). In this case, the differential vocabulary seems to acknowledge the different social roles that the men and women play—that is, when the sun is out men are probably working outside the home and women are probably working within it. So, when speakers of either language enter into a discourse situation, these gender categories guide how the speech act unfolds differentially—depending on whether the interlocutors are of the same gender, or of mixed gender. As Fleming (2012: 295) discovered in his survey of discourse in Koasati and other Native languages, there was a "remarkable complementarity of semantic gender, as a category of denotation, and social gender, as an aspect of identity indexed in discourse, in particular as these overlap in cases of gender deixis."

Dell Hymes (1971), as we saw, argued that discourse was not independent of grammar. As linguists started looking at conversations and utterances after Hymes' pivotal work, it became apparent that communication itself subserved broader cognitive processes. By the end of the 1970s, this awareness led to the cognitive linguistic movement. As mentioned previously, the most prominent early figure in the movement was the American linguist George Lakoff (Lakoff, 1987; Lakoff and Johnson, 1980). As we shall see in Chapter 6, Lakoff argued that the foundations of discourse were figurative, not literal. If we take words in isolation, then they can be constrained to literal meaning. However, when they are used in conversations they branch out figuratively, reaching into domains of meaning that are culture-specific. In other words, language impels speakers to construe the world in certain ways as they speak. As Pavlenko (2005: 435) has observed, "speakers' constructions of the world may be influenced by the structural patterns of their language." Similarly, Brown and Gullberg (2011: 80) remark that "fundamental cross-linguistic differences in lexicalization patterns have consequences for how events are construed or linguistically conceptualized, that is for what information speakers of a language consider as relevant and therefore select for expression."

Dan Slobin (1996: 79) provides many examples of how discursive relativity unfolds. For example, the sentence "The boy fell out and the dog was being chased by the bees" involves perfective verb tenses. On the other hand, in Spanish the same situation is described with perfective and imperfective verb expressions to indicate punctuality: "*Se cayó el niño y le perseguían al perro las avispas*" ("The boy fell and the wasps chased the dog"). Extending his analysis to German and Hebrew, Slobin notes that these languages "do not require speakers to attend to this contrast:" "*Der Junge fällt vom Baum runter und die Bienen gehen hinter dem Hund her*" (German, "The boys fall down from the tree and the bees go after the dog"); "*Hu nafal ve hakelev barax*" (Hebrew, "He fell and the dog ran away"). Slobin concludes that the organization of utterances in discourse is guided by grammatical categories that produce relativity effects—different ways of envisioning the same type of situation.

Sapir (1921) had made a similar kind of argument—namely, that sentence grammar mirrored situational structure. Even changing the order of words in a sentence such as "The farmer kills the duckling (Kills the farmer the duckling)," or omitting any of the words ("Farmer, kill the duckling") in it, brings about a shift in "modality," as he called it, showing that word order is tied to situational order, not to any principle of abstract grammatical structure. Sapir showed, in fact, that 13 distinct concepts could be expressed with the words making up this simple sentence: "The sentence is the outgrowth of historical and of unreasoning psychological forces rather than of a logical synthesis of elements that have been clearly grasped in their individuality" (Sapir 1921: 87).

Translation

As discussed in previous chapters, one of the main counterarguments against the LRH was that any word, phrase, or sentence in one language can be translated into another, even if to varying degrees of fidelity. Whorf never claimed that mutual understanding among people of different languages is blocked; rather, that translation is actually an attempt *at* reaching such an understanding. But since translation is an act of interpretation, it will invariably involve cross-linguistic relativity effects. These are especially identifiable when mistranslations occur.

Recall from Chapter 4 the example of the misinterpretation of the word *value* on an English hotel sign composed by a native speaker of French. A few other examples of this type of mistranslation (from Crocker 2007) are:

1. *Pets are not allowed in the breakfast* (sign at a French hotel).
2. *Beware the weatherly swell* (sign in a Japanese camera shop).
3. *Pillows have firmness to take care of your cervicals* (sign in a Barcelona hotel).

In example (1), the translation anomaly results from a wrong prepositional choice. An acceptable English version would be: *Pets are not allowed at breakfast*. As we saw previously, prepositions are hardly meaning-neutral grammatical items; they reflect perceptions and various mental perspectives. In example (2), the incongruity results from using *swell* and *weatherly* to evoke a poetic style, as expected in Japanese in such a situation. An appropriate version would be: *Beware of bad weather*. In example (3), *cervicals* is construed to be a formal way of saying *neck*, in imitation of the formal lexical style expected in Spanish language signs. An appropriate English version would be: *Our pillows are firm to prevent neck strain*. These mistranslations show, overall, that the translators "thought out" each message in terms of their native linguistic habits, transferring these to their construction of the English signs.

TRANSLATION

Source language (SL): The language to be translated.

Target language (TL): The language into which the source language is to be translated.

Metaphrase: A literal, word-for-word, translation.

Paraphrase: Expressing the meaning of a message in one language using different words or linguistic categories to make it understandable in another language.

Mistranslations reveal how the "background linguistic system" of the translator's native language is the "guide" for the mental activity involved in the translation process. As Whorf (1940: 234) observed:

> It was found that the background linguistic system (in other words, the grammar) of each language is not merely a reproducing instrument for voicing ideas but rather is itself the shaper of ideas, the

program and guide for people's mental activity, for their analysis of impressions, for their synthesis of their mental stock in trade. Formulation of ideas is not an independent process, strictly rational in the old sense, but is part of a particular grammar and differs, from slightly to greatly, among different grammars.

Translation brings out how the "formulation of ideas" is not independent from the particular grammar, lexicon, discourse styles, and so on of the native language, guiding the translation process. To put it another way, the linguistic system of the native language is "calqued" onto the language to be translated, resulting in anomalies such as the ones above.

CALQUING IN TRANSLATION

Calques are phrases that have been translated literally. A classic example of a calque in English is the title by which the Russian novel *The Brothers Karamazov*, written by Fyodor Dostoyevsky, is known. We no longer realize that this is a calque from the Russian title. In proper English it should be *The Karamazov Brothers*, a word order that is reflected commonly in such parallel phrases as the *Smith Brothers*, the *Carpenter Brothers*, and so on.

Main Types

Phraseological: This is a calque whereby phrases, usually idiomatic, are translated word-for-word: for example, the Italian phrase *nascere con la camicia*, if translated literally in English, would result in the anomalous (and meaningless) phrase *to be born with a shirt*; the corresponding English idiom is *to be born with a silver spoon in one's mouth*.

Classificatory: This is a calque whereby a specific type of classification in the native language is assumed to be the same in the target language: for example, in Italian, the word *uva*, which is a mass noun, has no plural form; if translated for *grapes* with a plural form, *uve*, it would result in a conceptual incongruity to a native speaker of Italian.

Morphological: This is a calque whereby the inflection pattern of a word in the native language is transferred to the corresponding word in the target language: it can be seen, for example, in the transfer of plural inflection patterns to foreign nouns, such as *spaghetts*, rather than the native Italian form *spaghetti*.

Syntactic: This is a calque whereby a syntactic construction (or form) of the native language is mapped onto the target language: for example, the mistranslated sign above, *Pets are not allowed in the breakfast*, shows that the functional meanings of the preposition *en* in French were mapped onto the English sentence.

> *Semantic:* This is a calque whereby a semantic category in the native language is calqued onto the target language: an example is confusing the meaning of English *value* with French *valeur* (Chapter 4).
>
> *Pragmatic:* This is a calque whereby a discourse protocol in one language is assumed to apply to the target language: for example, the use of *ciao* to greet strangers in Italy is a pragmatic calque, since this form is reserved for greeting someone in a familiar way.

Calquing occurs unconsciously in translation and manifests itself systematically when speakers of different linguistic backgrounds communicate with each other. In one relevant study, Danesi and Rocci (2009) documented several instances of calquing in communicative exchanges between native and non-native speakers of English with varying degrees of proficiency, where English was the common language of such exchanges. In one interaction, they observed how the single English word *affair*, which is polysemic (having various meanings), became a distractor during a conversation. In English, the word can mean:

1. Something done or to be done (as in "They got their affairs in order")
2. A professional or public transaction (as in "affairs of state")
3. A social occurrence or event (as in "Their wedding was a big affair")
4. A romantic or sexual relationship (as in "Theirs was a steamy affair").

Of the two speakers involved, A and B, A was a non-native speaker who had studied English as a second language in school, and B was a native speaker of English. During the conversation, at one point, A was asked by B: "Can you help me out?" A made the following response:

> "I am involved in an affair right now, and thus cannot help you out."

Upon hearing this statement, speaker B reacted by interpreting *affair* in terms of meaning (4), rather than meaning (1), since the way the statement was put together suggested this meaning to him. So, B assumed that A was caught up in a romantic tryst and, because of this situation, would not be able to help him out. The reason given by A seemed bizarre to B, since in normal English parlance it is unlikely that a romantic affair would be given as an excuse for opting out of something; but it was nevertheless accepted by B as A's genuine excuse because of the way in which it was phrased. The conversation ended with B uttering the following:

> "Well, I'm happy for you. I hope it works out."

This type of unwitting calque had no negative consequences in this case. However, it could potentially have had them if B sought a more concrete explanation, believing perhaps that the romantic tryst involved him in some way. In other conversations, A, whose native language was Italian, made the following remarks, showing different types of calquing:

1. "You carry your years very well" ("You are very young-looking").
2. "I have new informations for you" ("I have news for you").
3. "Amelia, my greetings to you" ("Amelia, how are you?").

In example (1), the speaker assumed that the Italian expression *portare bene gli anni* (literally, "to carry one years well") was transferable to English in a literal word-for-word metaphrasal way; this is an example of a phraseological calque. In example (2), the word *information* was treated like a count noun, as it is in Italian, whereas it is a mass noun in English and hence its anomalous pluralization; it is an example of a combination of morphological and classificatory calquing. Example (3) shows a pragmatic anomaly—namely, addressing someone with a polite form of speech, rather than an informal one.

Calquing provides evidence of how the source native language imprints itself on the target language—that is, how habits of thought, coded by the native language, influence the way in which the translator perceives the message to be translated. Successful translation occurs when the translator can move from one system of linguistic habits to the other, mapping the two via relevant linguistic structures. Bilinguals who are proficient in both their languages are largely capable of doing this, even though the occasional calquing occurs unwittingly.

Cross-linguistic analyses can pinpoint which areas are more or less subject to calquing. For instance, speakers of Australian Aboriginal languages imagine space as coexisting in relation to the speaker (Levinson 1996; Boroditsky 2009). So, in place of terms such as *left*, *right*, *backward*, and *forward*, they would use direction terms: *north*, *south*, *east*, and *west*. Consequently, speakers who are unaware of these patterns might produce the following utterances in English: "There is a spot on your northeast arm," or "The rock is to the south southwest." The greeting protocol "hello" would be rendered as "Where are you going?", or "Where are you coming from?" A response may be "To the northeast." Speakers would similarly indicate a location as "north of the house," rather than "in front of the house." The Australian languages predispose speakers to imagine relations in the world as oriented in space, which comes out in such calques.

Even concepts that seem to be directly translatable involve calquing. Take the example of time-telling, which would appear to be located near the 0 point on the Whorfian Scale; but it still requires some conceptual adjustment. For instance, in Italy, when someone says the equivalent of "See you at 5.00 pm," the tendency is to use the 24-hour clock—"*Ci vediamo alle 17*". This is not just a synonymous way of relating the same information; it involves the perception of time in a culturally-based fashion. The "feel" of the Italian expression is thus different from that of the corresponding English expression. A translation such as "See you at seventeen hundred hours," would be perceived as anomalous in normal conversations (see also Hyde 1993).

Translation shows that *equivalence* between languages is as adequate as need be—hence the constant use of paraphrasing in going from one language to the other, which is not an equivalence-based process. Problems of equivalence-rendering are especially marked when the grammars involved are typologically diverse—agglutinative-versus-isolating, for instance (Chapter 1). Translators in such cases are faced with the task of recreating culture-specific mental perspectives through the medium of their own native languages. This is especially true in the translation of perspectives built into metaphorical discourse. How would one translate *on a wild goose chase* or *tip of the iceberg* in some language that is vastly different historically from English?

The foregoing discussion has implications for studying the LRH in the domain of foreign language learning. Does the native language (NL) imprint itself on the learning of the foreign language (FL)? Is figurative language impossible to acquire in the FL? What does foreign language learning imply with regard to relativity effects between the two languages? As Kecskes (2000), Gentner, and others (Christie and Gentner 2012; Gentner 2003) have cogently argued, relativity differences are especially observable in the anomalous attempts at discourse that students manifest commonly, but which, when finally mastered, lead to an augmentation of cognition.

The augmentation process takes time to occur because of interference from the NL into the learning process. The process can be described in terms of three levels: (1) *equivalence*, whereby the forms of the NL and FL encode virtually the same conceptual structures; (2) *overlapping*, by which the forms have overlapping domains of meaning and use; and (3) *differentiated*, whereby the forms encompass differentiated conceptual domains. The control of these three levels at a high level of proficiency (if truly realizable) would clearly recalibrate how a learner would come to understand the world. A case of equivalence can be seen, for example, between the word *car* in English and *macchina* in Italian, but this, too, would impel the learner to understand differences that occur at the level of cultural interpretation, since an Italian *macchina* evokes different perceptions than does an American *car*. Equivalence is thus rare. Even among phylogenetically related languages (for example, English and German), it is exceptional to find concepts covering the same stretches of meaning exactly. More than likely, there will be some overlap between the conceptual domains. Needless to say, differentiated concepts are the hardest to acquire—for example, grasping the uses of the Italian subjunctive by an English-speaking student, given that the subjunctive has largely disappeared from the English language (except in some specific usages), is an example of an area where conceptual differentiation is inevitable. When these three dimensions are acquired by the FL learner and practiced in immersion contexts, habits of thought become augmented, leading to bilingualism at a high level.

Machine Translation

The foregoing discussion suggests that translation is a means for people to understand each other, despite relativity effects. Translators are key figures in the world of international and intercultural relations, since it is they who could destroy or create understanding between nations through translation. As Paul Auster (2007: ix) has aptly observed: "Translators are the shadow heroes of literature, the often forgotten instruments that make it possible for different cultures to talk to one another, who have enabled us to understand that we all, from every part of the world, live in one world."

Another way to examine translation as a means to test the LRH is to consider how a machine might be used for translation purposes, known as Machine Translation (MT)—an area that has received surprisingly little attention among researchers of the LRH. There are three main types of MT: (1) machine-aided translation—that is, translation carried out by a human translator who uses the computer as an ancillary or heuristic tool to help in the translation process; (2) human-aided machine translation—namely, the translation of an SL text by computer with a human translator editing the translation; and (3) fully-automated machine translation—that is, translation of the SL text solely by the computer without any human intervention.

MT goes back to the work of mathematician Warren Weaver and scientist Andrew D. Booth in the 1950s (Booth 1955; Booth and Locke 1955; Weaver 1955). The two researchers wrote the first scientific papers in the field, generating interest in it among scientists in various disciplines, including linguists. MT started with Weaver's efforts to adapt and modify the techniques of cryptanalysis during World War II into general principles of MT and the automated making of dictionaries. Given the low power of computers of the era, various problems emerged that almost shot down MT before it even got started. For instance, at Georgetown University in 1954, a widely publicized experiment involved the mistranslation of Russian sentences into English via MT. The results made it clear that autonomous MT lacked the kind of conceptual sophistication that humans have when it comes to tapping into the meanings of sentences. A classic example from the experiment was the mistranslation of "The spirit is willing, but the flesh is weak" into Russian as "The vodka is strong, but the meat is rotten." Clearly, the problem of translating figurative language emerged early on as a complex one for MT to resolve.

So, too, was that of polysemy. In 1960, the linguist Yehoshua Bar-Hillel looked at polysemic aspects of MT, producing what came to be known as the Bar-Hillel paradox. The main problem with MT, Bar-Hillel argued, was that humans use extra-linguistic information to make sense of messages and that computers cannot access this in the same way that humans do. In other words, context is a determinant in how humans understand language and interpret meanings. He illustrated the paradox with the following examples:

1. "The pen is in the box" (= the writing instrument is in the container).
2. "The box is in the pen" (= the container is inside another container, a playpen).

Speakers of English can easily distinguish between the two because they have access to outside information about the meaning of the word *pen*. A computer (in that era) did not and thus would produce anomalies. Bar-Hillel's paradox led shortly thereafter to the serious study of extra-linguistic inferences in human discourse. In order for a fully automatic MT system to process such sentences correctly, it would have to have some algorithm that would indicate that *pens* as writing instruments are (typically) smaller than boxes; that boxes understood as containers are smaller than *pens* (typically, again); and that it is impossible for a bigger object to be contained by a smaller one. This kind of understanding involves extra-linguistic knowledge gained from experience.

MT has since made great advances that have led to effective systems today, such as Google Translate. These deal with polysemy and other ambiguities in statistical terms, whereby the algorithm is designed to make inferences about the appropriate meaning to be selected in terms of the frequency distribution measures of a lexical item in large amounts of relevant data. The idea is to simulate the human use of real-world information in resolving polysemy, on the basis of probability metrics. The algorithm searches for analogous or isomorphic forms and converts them into options for the system. The details of how this is done are somewhat complex, and they need not concern us here. Suffice it to say that the computer processing of linguistic meaning involves mining data from millions of texts on the Internet, analyzing them statistically in terms of linguistic categories, and then classifying them for the algorithmic modeling of polysemy through frequency analysis. The technique goes back to the founder of information theory, Claude Shannon (1948), who asked the question: "Given a sequence of letters, such as the sequence *for ex...*, what is the likelihood of the next letter?" A probability distribution to answer this question can be easily derived given a frequency history of letters following this sequence: $a = 0.4$, $b = 0.00001$, and so on, where the probabilities of all the "next letters" sum to 1.0.

In this approach, the probability of a word is computed by determining the presence of variables such as the following:

1. The position of a word in a text.
2. The linguistic features typically associated with the topic or theme of the text, which involves specific kinds of grammatical and lexical choices given the networks and circuitry that words entail.
3. Syntactic considerations involving the likelihood that a certain structure will follow or precede others.

But the problem of culture-specific meaning and cross-linguistic interpretation still remains, which is at the core of the translation equivalence problem. Calling someone a *Casanova* or a *Don Juan*, rather than a *ladykiller*, evokes an array of socially significant connotations that an algorithm cannot possibly grasp. Nevertheless, MT can be used to shed light on the implications of translation errors, as Yair Neuman (2014: 61) points out:

> The reason for using MT is twofold. First, there is no better way to understand the loss accompanying translation than by examining the most structured and formal attempt of translation known today. Second, instead of pointing at the problems and errors of MT, I suggest using it in order to better understand cultural peculiarities and discrepancies. The second suggestion is somewhat counterintuitive as we positively think of eliminating errors and solving problems. Sometimes, however, errors can be used for the better.

Advances in computer technology have led to very efficient MT systems with high fidelity translation results. An SL text is parsed into an internal representation, much like the ones used in linguistic grammars. Then, a transfer mechanism adapts this representation to the TL text, applying statistically obtained contextual information through frequency analyses, which allow the algorithm to make inferences about the appropriate meaning of a lexical item, or a syntactic structure in the TL. One of the most effective systems is Google Translate which, in 2016, announced that it would use a so-called "neural MT engine," with the ability to translate whole sentences at a time, using extra-linguistic data analysis to help it figure out the most relevant translation. But, like any MT system, there are limitations. In fact, it often delivers inaccurate translations, which need to be rectified by human translators. For example it has shown difficulties differentiating between perfective and imperfective verb tenses, as encoded in Romance languages such as Spanish, Italian, and French. Treatment of the subjunctive mood or counterfactuals is also problematic, as is the ability to implement pragmatic strategies, such as formal versus informal speech in a culturally appropriate way.

In sum, the work on MT has produced two general implications with regard to the LRH: (1) machines cannot penetrate the internal meaning structure of language forms easily, many of which delve into the culture-specific aspects built into a language; and (2) while translation is possible, it is always approximate and never equivalent, mirroring what happens in human-based translation. Moreover, where meanings are figurative, the translation process becomes increasingly more difficult.

Epilogue

Since translatability involves comprehensibility, it holds many implications for studying the LRH. It is interesting to note that the 2016 movie *Arrival* introduced the LRH to a broad audience. The story revolves around a linguist, Louise Banks, who is given the task of communicating with extraterrestrial visitors who have landed on earth. The following stretch of dialogue between Banks and one of her colleagues, Ian Donnelly, is a relevant one, since it imaginatively encapsulates the main theme of this chapter.

> *IAN DONNELLY:* Language is the foundation of civilization. It is the glue that holds a people together. It is the first weapon drawn in a conflict....Like their ship or their bodies, their written language has no forward or backward direction. Linguists call this "non-linear orthography," which raises the question, Is this how they think?...If you immerse yourself into a foreign language, then you can actually rewire your brain.
> *LOUISE BANKS:* Yeah, the Sapir-Whorf hypothesis. It's the theory that the language you speak determines how you think and...
> *IAN DONNELLY:* Yeah, it affects how you see everything.

The problem that Banks faces is a Whorfian one—even if she could devise a set of symbols that the aliens could decipher, they would be imbued with human meanings and thus are unlikely to be understood by the alien species. She would not, in effect, know how they think and what they would make of our linguistic symbols. Words are capsules of thought derived from human experiences. They are not just devices carrying information;

they encode interpretations and evaluations of the world. So, Banks cannot be sure what interpretation a linguistic signal or cue will elicit in the aliens (if any). The movie, however, is optimistic, showing that Bank's attempts at "astrolinguistic communication" (Ollongren 2012) reflects our own attempts to understand each other. The assumption is that the alien species would understand the same kind of information that humans do, which is an unlikely supposition. Moreover, even if the information packed into single units of language can be somehow translated into an alien code, the use of these in discourse with the aliens would be an impracticable communicative task, given the nature and function of discourse in human life, as discussed in this chapter (Sherzer 1987).

How would an alien, or a machine for that matter, understand allusions to historical or culture-specific events or themes in discourse? The term used to designate how discourse generates meaning by allusion, inference, implication, or suggestion to other texts is *intertexuality*. For example, citations from, or allusions to, Biblical figures, events, and sayings figure prominently in Christian religious discourse; on the other hand, allusions to famous acts of criminal violence by prisoners are part of a generic prison discourse. Some allusions and texts are especially critical for the discourse community. For example, Martin Luther King Jr.'s speeches are important in the political discourse connected to social justice, while citations from Shakespeare are intrinsic to various aspects of English literary criticism discourse. Knowledge of these referential canons implies a specific form of world savvy. A scientist interacting with a colleague may refer to something that was presented recently at a conference they both attended, in order to discuss its implications. This type of intertextuality allows them to acknowledge that they belong to the same realm of shared understanding and knowledge.

Again: How would an alien or a computer ever grasp the meaning of such allusions? The notion of intertextuality was introduced by semiotician Roland Barthes (1977) and elaborated subsequently by Julia Kristeva (1980). For Barthes, a text is constituted by bits of codes, various conventional formulas, and specific kinds of discourses, all of which pass into the text and are reconfigured within it—it is thus, a blend of unconscious quotations, without quotation marks. For Kristeva, a text is more than the result of a single author's efforts—it is the result of other texts converging on it through the author's own unconscious memory.

Discussion Questions and Activities

Chapter Questions

1. Do discourse practices produce relativity effects? Do they guide social behaviors?

2. What does translation reveal about linguistic relativity?
3. What can we learn from studying Machine Translation vis-à-vis linguistic relativity?

Related Questions

4. If you have learned a foreign language, do you recall any systematic errors that you made (or continue to make) that are attributable to calquing? If so, which ones?
5. What aspects of Machine Translation reveal the uniqueness of human language?
6. Intertextuality implies that people often refer to culture-specific references or allusions when talking either consciously (by direct reference), or unconsciously (by allusion). What are some examples of *intertexts* in everyday English discourse? If you know another language, are similar intertexts available to the speaker or not?
7. If perception and knowledge are tied to reference (the use of signs), will it ever be possible to know the "truth" about the world? Explain your answer.
8. Discuss the idea that verbal communication is potentially a dangerous act. Do you agree or disagree? What does it imply in Whorfian terms?

Activities

1. How would you phrase the following speech acts in English? If you know another language, translate them into that language and discuss the translations.
   (a) Invite your employer to dinner.
   (b) Invite a friend to dinner.
   (c) Tell a child to put something dangerous down.
   (d) Tell an adult to put something dangerous down.
2. Discuss the cultural meanings of the following food items in English. Translate them into another language, comparing the meanings, connecting them to typical ways of speaking about them.
   (a) bread
   (b) milk
   (c) apple
   (d) fig
   (e) peach
   (f) cake.

3. Identify the contexts in which each statement might be uttered. Does changing the context change the meaning? If you know another language how would these be translated?
   (a) Really?
   (b) It's not true.
   (c) My friend lives in Italy.
   (d) Tell me all that you know.
   (e) Quiet!
   (f) What time is it?
   (g) My name is Alexander.
4. Explain the implications in social terms that each title entails.
   (a) Mr.
   (b) Mrs.
   (c) Miss
   (d) Ms.
   (e) Professor
   (f) Doctor
   (g) Sir
   (h) Madam.
5. Provide an appropriate verbal script for carrying out each of the following social functions. What do they tell us about the link between the language and the functions? How would you render these in another language you may know?
   (a) Asking a policeman directions to find a street
   (b) Answering the phone
   (c) Making an appointment with a doctor
   (d) Asking a bank teller to make a deposit
   (e) Inviting someone you met recently to get a bite to eat.

6

FIGURATIVE LANGUAGE

Prologue

In the late 1970s, the expanding interest of research on figurative language in linguistics led to a new paradigm in the field: *cognitive linguistics*. Today, this term has two main designations. It refers to: (1) (as in its initial designation), the study of figurative meaning, and especially metaphor, in language and discourse, and (2) any approach to the relation between language and cognition. In this chapter, the term is used in the first sense, since this is the relevant one for examining the LRH, and it is the one that is most compatible with current research paradigms in linguistic anthropology.

It is somewhat surprising to find that Whorf did not see metaphor as consequential to the study of his own hypothesis. He claimed, for instance, that Hopi had fewer figurative devices than did SAE languages, in contrast to his main critic, Malotki (1983) who, instead, saw Hopi conceptualizations of time and space as based on such devices. Interestingly, Whorf does allude (perhaps unwittingly) to the importance of a feature of figurative language—*synesthesia*—or the identification of the properties of one sensory mode in terms of another (Whorf 1956: 155):

> Synesthesia, or suggestion by certain sense receptions of characters belonging to another sense, as of light and color by sounds and vice versa, should be made more conscious by a linguistic metaphorical system that refers to nonspatial experiences by terms for spatial ones, though undoubtedly it arises from a deeper source. Probably in the first instance metaphor arises from synesthesia and not the reverse; yet metaphor need not become firmly rooted in linguistic pattern, as Hopi shows.

As George Lakoff (1987: 325), a key figure in the cognitive linguistic movement, pointed out, Whorf's ideas sometimes appear to be inconsistent, especially as they refer to metaphor. Whorf even seemed to believe that the abundant presence of metaphor in SAE languages was a weakness in them (Whorf 1941):

> Our metaphorical system, by naming nonspatial experiences after spatial ones, imputes to sounds, smells, tastes, emotions, and thoughts qualities like the colors, luminosities, shapes, angles, textures, and motions of spatial experience. And to some extent the reverse transference occurs; for, after much talking about tones as high, low, sharp, dull, heavy, brilliant, slow, the talker finds it easy to think of some factors in spatial experience as like factors of tone. Thus we speak of "tones" of color, a gray "monotone," a "loud" necktie, a "taste" in dress: all spatial metaphor in reverse. It may be that in this way our metaphorical language ... is in some sense a confusion of thought.

Whorf went on to maintain that Hopi was free of such "confusion of thought" (Whorf 1941):

> The absence of such metaphor from Hopi speech is striking. Use of space terms when there is no space involved is not there—as if on it had been laid the taboo teetotal! The reason is clear when we know that Hopi has abundant conjugational and lexical means of expressing duration, intensity, and tendency directly as such, and that major grammatical patterns do not, as with us, provide analogies for an imaginary space. The many verb "aspects" express duration and tendency of manifestations, while some of the "voices" express intensity, tendency, and duration of causes or forces producing manifestations. Then a special part of speech, the "tensors," a huge class of words, denotes only intensity, tendency, duration, and sequence. The function of the tensors is to express intensities, "strengths," and how they continue or vary, their rate of change; so that the broad concept of intensity, when considered as necessarily always varying and/or continuing, includes also tendency and duration. Tensors convey distinctions of degree, rate, constancy, repetition, increase and decrease of intensity, immediate sequence, interruption or sequence after an interval, etc., also qualities of strengths, such as we should express metaphorically as smooth, even, hard, rough.

Despite his strange view of metaphor as being absent in Hopi, the above citation could have easily been written by a cognitive linguist today to describe metaphorical cognition in Hopi—all that has to be done is to replace his term *tensor* with the term *metaphor*, since they seem to allude to the same cognitive phenomenon. Paradoxically, perhaps in no other area of research has the work on metaphor in cognitive linguistics been so supportive of the LRH.

The starting point for cognitive linguistics is Lakoff and Johnson's book *Metaphors We Live By* (1980); in it Lakoff and Johnson provided a theory of linguistic meaning that continues to have implications for studying the LRH to this day. Their main claim is that there are two levels of metaphor—the linguistic and the conceptual. For instance, the statement "He's a snake" is a linguistic metaphor, if considered in isolation. However, if considered more generically, it can be seen to be a token of a more abstract metaphorical concept—*people are animals*. Lakoff and Johnson called this a *conceptual metaphor*, seeing it as the source of other related linguistic metaphors based on it—"He's a gorilla," "He's a bear," "He's an eagle," and so on. The two scholars go on to illustrate meticulously the presence of conceptual metaphors in everyday discourse, thus disavowing the mainstream view at the time that metaphorical utterances were alternatives to literal ways of speaking or exceptional categories of language. According to the latter view, speakers would purportedly try out a literal interpretation first when they heard statements such as the ones above, choosing a metaphorical one only when a literal interpretation was not possible from the context. But, as Lakoff and Johnson convincingly argued, this is hardly consistent with what actually goes on in people's minds as they speak. When a sentence such as "The murderer was an animal" is uttered, virtually no one will interpret it literally. Only if told that the *animal* was non-human, would a speaker assign it a literal meaning, but even then the word *murderer* would have metaphorical resonance, since it is a human concept that is applied in this case to a non-human animal.

This chapter will discuss the work on figurative language, which has had numerous implications for studying cognition, culture, and the LRH since the 1980s (for example, Kövecses 1986, 1988, 1990). The questions that will guide the discussion are the following:

1. How is figurative language interconnected with cognition?
2. How does metaphor manifest itself in language and discourse?
3. Does figurative language guide actions and behaviors?

Conceptual Metaphor Theory

In cognitive linguistics, metaphor is defined as a neural process involving the blending of two seemingly disparate referents into a singular thought. For example, in the linguistic metaphor "The professor is a snake," there are two referents that are related to each other as follows:

- There is a primary referent, the *professor*, which is known as the *topic* of the metaphor.
- Then there is a secondary referent, the *snake*, which is known as the *vehicle* of the metaphor.

- When these are amalgamated, a singular meaning, called the *ground*, emerges. In this case it constitutes a portrayal of the personality of the professor in terms of a serpentine image.

The process of linking the two referents never produces a denotative (literal) meaning but, rather, one that is highly connotative. In the example above, this involves culture-specific interpretations of, and reactions to, snakes—"slyness," "danger," "slipperiness," and so on. It is this interrelated set of connotations that is embedded in the metaphor. The question now becomes: Is there any psychological motivation for this? In the case of "The professor is a snake," the probable reason for connecting two seemingly unrelated referents seems to be the perception that humans and animals are linked in some existential way—a linkage that is expressed with the general conceptual formula, *people are animals*, as mentioned.

Although experimental research on metaphor goes back to the last part of the nineteenth century, and was studied in detail by the Gestalt psychologists in the 1950s and 1960s (for example, Asch 1950, 1958), it was not until several key works in the late 1970s and early 1980s that it laid the groundwork for a new approach to the study of language—the works included a 1977 study by Pollio, Barlow, Fine, and Pollio, *The Poetics of Growth: Figurative Language in Psychology, Psychotherapy, and Education*; a 1979 collection of papers by Andrew Ortony, *Metaphor and Thought*; a 1980 anthology put together by Richard P. Honeck and Robert R. Hoffman, *Cognition and Figurative Language*; and the 1980 book by George Lakoff and Mark Johnson, *Metaphors We Live By*. The term *conceptual metaphor theory* (CMT) emerged to characterize the new approach. The central premise of CMT is that figurative meaning pervades language and discourse; it is not a part of rhetorical style but, rather, a building block of linguistic thought (Boroditsky 2000; Lakoff 1987). In the conceptual metaphor above, *people* is called the *target domain*, because it is the general topic (the "target" of the conceptual metaphor); and *animals* is the *source domain*, because it represents the set of vehicles that deliver the metaphor (the "source" of the metaphorical ground). Source domains for a concept are not mutually exclusive; rather, they are intertwined in a conceptual network. For instance, the source domain for conceptualizing *personality* is not limited to animals; it can be based on *tactility* ("The professor is a softie"), *electricity* ("The professor is always wired"), *matter* ("The professor is a rock"), and so on. Each source domain implies a different connotative portrayal of personality.

The psychological mechanism behind conceptual metaphors was called an *image schema* by Lakoff and Johnson (Johnson 1987; Lakoff 1987). This converts physical, affective, and other kinds of concrete experiences into source domains for understanding specific kinds of abstractions. For example, the physical experience of orientation—*up* versus *down*, *back* versus *front*, *near* versus *far*, and so on—produces an image schema in the brain underlying how we commonly conceptualize such abstractions as *happiness* ("Lately my spirits are up"), *time* ("This goes considerably back in time"), *affection* ("We are really close to each other"), among many others. The physical knowledge of containers underlies another kind of image schema that produces conceptualizations such as those related to the *mind* ("My mind is full of good memories"), *emotions* ("My heart is filled with hope"), and so on. However, this does not mean that all language is metaphorical. As Lakoff (2012) has observed, while metaphor is basic to cognition, literal meaning is not absent from language:

> Although the old literal-metaphorical distinction was based on assumptions that have proved to be false, one can make a different sort of literal-metaphorical distinction: those concepts that are not comprehended via conceptual metaphor might be called literal. Thus, while a great many common concepts like causation and purpose are metaphorical, there is nonetheless an extensive range of nonmetaphorical concepts. So, sentences such as *The balloon went up* and *The cat is on the mat* are not metaphorical; they are designed to describe concrete physical referents; but the instant one moves away from such modes of reference and starts talking about abstractions or emotions, metaphorical understanding is the norm.

Lakoff and Johnson (1980) also claimed in their ground-breaking work, that metonymy and irony, while figurative in meaning, are distinct structurally and conceptually from metaphor. Metonymy is the process of representing a concept with something that is associated with it: "She loves Hemingway" (the writings of Hemingway); "The automobile is destroying our health" (the collection of automobiles); and so on. In parallel with the notion of conceptual metaphor, the term conceptual metonym has been adopted to refer to generalized concepts based on metonymy, rather than metaphor: *the face for the person* ("He's nothing more than another pretty face"); *a body part for the person* ("Get your butt over here!"); and so on. As in metaphor, experience and context play a role in metonymic constructs. Irony is defined as a strategy whereby words are used to convey a meaning contrary to their literal sense in a specific context—for example, "I love being tortured" would be interpreted as ironic if it were uttered by someone experiencing unwelcome pain. The intent of speakers, including their prosody (tone of voice, accent, etc.), their relation to listeners, and the social context are all factors that establish the ironic meaning of an utterance. If the above sentence were uttered by a masochist, then it would hardly have an ironic meaning.

> **TERMS FOR CMT**
>
> *Linguistic Metaphor:* Specific metaphorical expression, such as "You are a pussycat."
> *Conceptual Metaphor:* Thought formula on which linguistic metaphors are based: *people are animals.*
> *Metonymy:* Using the part of something to represent the whole or vice versa (called *synecdoche*): "There are too many suits around here" (business people).
> *Irony:* Referring to something in contrastive or opposite ways to emphasize the meaning: "What a great day" (uttered during a hurricane).

Metaphor allows us to grasp abstractions in experiential and culture-specific ways, shaping how we see certain sectors of reality. By portraying *life* as a *stage*, for example, the English language has mapped the experience of what takes place on stages onto life in general—"Life is a comedy," "Life is a farce," and so on. By conceiving of *life* through the image schema of a *stage*, we are also implying that *stages* are *life*—what happens on a stage is thus construed as telling us what happens in real life, at the same time that what happens in real life is suggested to us by the experience of the theater. In other words, the two parts of a conceptual metaphor—the target and source—are suggestive of each other (Danesi 2017b).

Mark Johnson (1987) provided an insightful description of how image schemata work psychologically. For instance, the containment schema reflects how the sense of space is lexicalized in specific ways. Consider the lexeme *out*. In the examples below, it is used to imply that someone or something leaves a spatially bounded landmark:

1. She went *out* of the room.
2. He got *out* of the car.
3. Our dog jumped *out* of the pen.

The same word could be used to indicate a mass that spreads externally from the containing landmark:

1. Your friend poured *out* the beans.
2. Roll *out* the carpet.
3. Send *out* the troops.

The containment image schema unites these different referents conceptually. Actually, spatially-based image schemata abound in language. Consider the following utterances:

1. You should *think over* carefully what you just said.
2. When did you *think up* that preposterous idea?
3. You should *think out* the entire problem.
4. Have you *thought through* that idea?
5. I cannot *think straight* any more.

These expressions are the result of image schemata that connect ideas to objects and their movement through space. The metaphor *think up* elicits a mental image of upward movement, portraying an idea as an object extracted physically from a kind of mental terrain; *think over* evokes the image of scanning ideas with the mind's eye; *think out* elicits an image of extracting an idea so that it can be held up to the scrutiny of the mind's eye; *think straight* produces an image of sequential, and thus logical, movement of an idea from one point to another via a straight linear path; and *think through* generates an image of continuous, unbroken movement through space. This image schematic system allows speakers to locate and identify abstract ideas in relation to spatiotemporal contexts, although such contexts are purely imaginary. It transforms the physiology of vision into a physiology of thinking.

In current versions of CMT, image schemata are seen as the connective mechanisms between experiences in different regions of the brain. The result is now called a *blend*. Recall the orientation image schema. In a metaphor such as "Prices are always going up," the two neural regions involved are the one where quantity is processed (*prices*) and another where verticality is processed (*going up*). Lakoff (2011) explains such linkages as embedded in the "metaphorical circuitry" of the brain:

> Perhaps most remarkable, there appear to be brain structures that we are born with that provide pathways ready for metaphor circuitry. Edward Hubbard has observed that critical brain regions coordinating space and time measurement are adjacent in the brain, making it easy for the universal metaphors for understanding space in terms of time to develop (as in "Christmas is coming" or "We're coming up on Christmas.") Mirror neuron pathways linking brain regions coordinating vision and hand actions provide a natural pathway for the conceptual metaphor that *Seeing Is Touching* (as in "Their eyes met").

Idealized Cognitive Models

Blending manifests itself in higher-order conceptualizations that link different source domains, producing what Lakoff (1987) calls *idealized cognitive models* (ICMs). For example, source domains delivering the notion of *ideation* (how ideas, theories, and other such abstract constructs are understood) include the following:

- *sight* ("I cannot *see* what you are saying")
- *geometry* ("The views of Plato and Descartes are *parallel* in many ways")
- *plants* ("That theory has *deep roots* in philosophy")
- *buildings* ("Your theory is *well-constructed*")
- *food* ("That is an *appetizing* idea")
- *fashion* ("His theory went out of *style* years ago")
- *persons* ("Those ideas have *long legs*")
- *commodities* ("You must *package* your ideas differently").

When linked, these source domains constitute an ICM of *ideation*. This then becomes the conceptual network that can be used for delivering the concept of *ideation* in discourse and other expressive activities.

The structure of ICMs shows two general configurations, which can be called *clustering* and *radiative* (Danesi 2020). The *ideation* ICM is an example of a clustering system, whereby source domains cluster around a target domain, shown in Figure 6.1.

When the topic of *ideas* comes up in a certain interactive situation, speakers of English may deliver it by navigating conceptually through the various source domains that cluster around it according to need, whim, or

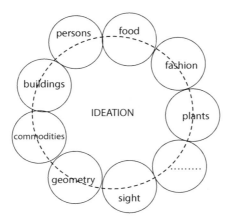

FIGURE 6.1 The clustering system of an ideation ICM

situation. For example, the sentence, "I can't see why that idea is not well-known, given that it has deep historical roots and is theoretically on solid ground," has been put together with three of the above source domains (sight, plants, and buildings).

ICM clusters have implications for the LRH in terms of which domains are culture-specific and which are not. For example, several of the source domains for the above ICM—*food, people,* and *sight*—are relatively understandable across cultures. That is, people from non-English-speaking cultures could easily figure out what linguistic metaphors based on these domains mean if they were translated or relayed to them. However, there are some source domains that are more likely to be culture-specific—such as, for instance, the *commodities* domain—and thus beyond smooth cross-cultural comprehension. This suggests that there may be different categories of conceptual metaphors, some of which are more common in languages across the world than others. The *ideas are food* concept, for example, is a basic or root metaphor because it connects a universal physical process (eating) to an abstraction (thinking) directly. But the *ideas are commodities* concept reveals a more culture-specific abstraction.

The second type of ICM can be called *radiative*, since it shows a single source domain "radiating outwards" to deliver different target domains. For example, the *plant* source domain above not only allows us to conceptualize *ideas* ("That idea has deep ramifications"), but other target domains, such as *love* ("Their love is deeply rooted"), *influence* ("Your influence is sprouting throughout academia"), *success* ("My career has borne great fruit), *knowledge* ("Science has many branches"), *wisdom* ("Wisdom blossoms from experience), and *friendship* ("Our friendship is starting to bud"), among others. The structure of this type of ICM is shown in Figure 6.2.

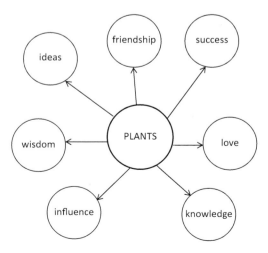

FIGURE 6.2 The radiative system of an ideation ICM

Radiative structure reveals the tendency to envisage some abstract concepts as implicating each other through a specific associative frame of reference (source domain). It explains why we talk of seemingly different things, such as wisdom and friendship, with the same metaphorical vehicles. Clustering, on the other hand, explains why we use different vehicles to deliver the same concept.

There are problems of psychological realism with ICM theory, as has been pointed out. As Dafina Genova (2003: 129) observes, with this theory, the "old controversy for realism or cognitivism in science, respectively in linguistics, is again brought to the fore." However, research exists that is highly supportive of ICM theory. For example, Hubbard, Arman, Ramachandran, and Boynton (2005) have shown that mathematical abstractions such as the Cartesian plane emerge from associating source domains of various kinds, clustering around a central idea. Research has also suggested that ICMs double back on speakers to affect their experiences of reality, such as pain and illness. Consider the following clustering source domains in English related to the target domain of health:

The body is a machine

1. My body isn't working. Can it be fixed?
2. Your heart has a malfunction.
3. Some of my organs are breaking down.

Disease is war

4. We must fight back against cancer.
5. She has been combatting liver disease for years.
6. I finally beat cancer.

Treatment is a battle

7. We must destroy those cells first.
8. We will use all weapons at our disposal against diabetes.
9. We must attack the disease with all our might.

In one relevant study, Casarett, Pickard, Fishman, Alexander, Arnold, Pollak, and Tulsky (2010) found that physicians unconsciously used source domains such as those above in diagnostic interactions around two-thirds of the time. Examining patient reactions, the researchers found that doctors who used them effectively were seen as better communicators by patients, reporting that they were able to grasp the implications of their disease and its symptomatology much more tangibly. The use of the *cancer is war* conceptual metaphor in diagnostic situations seems to have particular therapeutic resonance in Western societies, given its diffusion in everyday language.

As Lakoff (2012: 163–164) has implied throughout his work, studies such as these are not surprising, because ICMs are perceived as real: "metaphors can be made real in less obvious ways as well, in physical symptoms, social institutions, social practices, laws, and even foreign policy and forms of discourse and of history." To expand upon what Lakoff means, consider the concept of *time* in English. Common source domains connected with *time* include *journey* ("There's a long way to go before it's over"), *substance* ("There's not enough time left to finish the task"), *moving person* ("Time comes and goes"), and *device* ("Time keeps ticking on"), among others. Now, these source domains are "made real" through representations such as mythical figures (*Father Time*), narratives (*The Time Machine* (1895) by H. G. Wells), and others.

In an early version of ICM theory, the formation of concepts was seen as a mapping process, whereby source domains were mapped onto target domains. Neurologically, this implies that the elements in one region of the brain are mapped onto the other via image schematic mechanisms. This view was eventually modified and called *blending*, as mentioned above (Fauconnier and Turner 2002). A blend is formed when the brain identifies distinct entities in different neural regions as the same entity in another neural region. Together, they constitute the blend. In the metaphor *fighting a war on cancer*, the two distinct entities are *cancer* and *fighting*. The blending process is guided by the inference that *disease is a war*, constituting the final touch to the blend—a touch that keeps the two entities distinct in different neural regions, while identifying them simultaneously as a single entity in the third one.

Guhe et al. (2011) have developed a computational model of how blending could be simulated. They devised a system by which different conceptualizations of number can be blended together to form new ones via recognition and combination of common features (Lakoff and Núñez 2000) The ideas are worked out using a so-called Heuristic-Driven Theory Projection (HDTP), a method based on higher-order metaphorical blending, allowing for commonalities to be established through the transfer of concepts from one domain to another, producing new conceptual blends.

The work on conceptual metaphors has, overall, reignited the universalist-versus-relativist debate. One of its critics is Steven Pinker who, in his 2007 book, *The Stuff of Thought* (Pinker 2007: 238–249), dismissed CMT outright, remarking that it was based on two specious notions—the "killjoy theory" and the "messianic theory." The former categorizes most metaphors as "dead," and then asserts that modern day speakers are not aware of the comparison made between source and target domains in these metaphors. The latter states that users of metaphors are aware of how they may work, and then uses this assumption to claim that perceptual experiences lead to complex thoughts. But in using these two terms, Pinker has himself used metaphorical thinking (*killjoy* and *messianic*) to dismiss CMT. Aware that he cannot completely avoid metaphor, Pinker settles on a compromise view that falls between the two theories as a way of acknowledging the presence of figurative cognition; but, ultimately, he postulates that they tell us little about the nature of what he called mentalese (Chapter 1), which, again, is itself a metaphor.

A more substantive critique is that CMT researchers seek metaphorical data in a "top-down" direction, looking for a few examples to construct conceptual metaphors, and then examining the structure of those metaphors in order to make theoretical proclamations. This may ignore the way language is actually used (Kövecses 2008; Slobin 2003). Moreover, there may be more going on in the brain than image schematic blending. In the early 1970s, before the advent of CMT, Melissa Bowerman (1973) had already connected conceptual development and language development, using cross-linguistic comparisons to disentangle what is possibly innate from what is learned. She showed that certain cognitive processes did not use language to any significant extent and therefore could not be subject to linguistic relativity. On the other hand, as we saw with Vygotsky (Chapter 2), metaphor is a poetic fable that children use as a strategy for filling in conceptual gaps.

Extensions

To reiterate here, a key aspect of metaphor is what Lakoff (above) characterized as being "made real" in many nonverbal systems, which are thus extensions of metaphorical thinking. One of these is gesture. David McNeill (1992), for instance, has shown that the gestures accompanying speech are hardly random; rather, they unconsciously reinforce the meanings in vocal utterances. After videotaping a large sample of people as they spoke, McNeill found that the gestures that accompany speech, which he called *gesticulants*, exhibit imagery that cannot be shown overtly via vocal speech. One type of gesticulant is based on metaphor. For example, McNeill observed a male speaker announcing that what he had just seen was a cartoon, simultaneously raising up his hands as if offering his listener a kind of object. He was not referring to the cartoon itself, but to the genre of the cartoon. His gesture represented this genre as if it were an object, placing it into an act of offering to the listener. This type of gesticulant typically accompanies utterances that contain metaphors such as "presenting an idea," "putting forth an idea," "offering advice," and so on, which instantiate the conceptual metaphor *ideas are conduits*.

Another extension can be seen in anthropomorphism, whereby the body is projected onto various domains of understanding. Here are some examples in English:

- a *body* of water
- the *body* of a work

- the *eye* of a storm
- the *eye* of the needle
- the *face* of a clock
- the *foot* of a mountain
- the *head* of a table
- the *head* of an organization
- the *head* of the household
- the *leg* of a race.

Anthropomorphism is present in vocabularies across the world. In the language spoken by the Batammaliba people, who live in the border region between the West African states of Togo and the Benin Republic, the parts of their houses are named with body terms, indicating that they perceive the house as an extension of the body (Tilley 1999: 41–49). Keith Basso (1990) examined anthropomorphism for naming automobile parts in the Western Apache language of east-central Arizona. He explained the use of metaphorical names as reflecting the fact that cars replaced horses in Apache life and, so, the words used to describe the anatomy of horses have been reapplied to describe cars. Moreover, since vehicles can generate and sustain locomotion by themselves, they are perceived as extensions of bodily locomotion and, thus, as having body parts.

In the Zapotec language, spoken in Oaxaca, Mexico, anthropomorphism reveals itself in a complex ICM system that ranges from concepts involving orientation to those involving space and the parts of things (MacLaury 1989) (see Table 6.1).

Another area in which metaphor is made real (as Lakoff put it) is in social rituals and symbols. As an example, consider the *love is a sweet taste* conceptual metaphor in English, which can be seen in such common

TABLE 6.1 Anthropomorphism in Zapotec

Concept	*Word Equivalent in English*
top	head
front	belly
upper front	face
lower front	foot
back	back
side	side
underneath	buttock
four-legged animal	hand
entrance	mouth
inside	stomach
outside	face

expressions as "She's my sweetheart," "They went on a honeymoon," and so on. The reifications of this conceptual metaphor can be found in rituals, symbols, and behaviors, such as giving sweets to a loved one on Valentine's day, symbolizing matrimonial love at a wedding ceremony with a cake, sweetening the breath with candy before kissing a paramour, and so on. These are all social-ritualistic-symbolic correlates of the same conceptual metaphor. In Chagga, a Bantu language of Tanzania, similar correlates exist. It is no coincidence that the language possesses the same conceptual metaphor. In Chagga, the man is perceived to be the *eater* and the woman his *sweet food*, as can be detected in expressions that mean, in translated form, "Does she taste sweet?" "She tastes sweet as sugar honey," and so on (Emantian 1995: 168).

Metaphor extends as well to the origins of proverbial language. A common expression such as "He has fallen from grace" would have been recognized instantly in a previous era as referring to the Adam and Eve story in the Bible. Today, we continue to use this proverbial expression with only a dim awareness (if any) of its Biblical origins. Expressions that portray *life as a journey*—"I'm still a long way from my goal," "There is no end in sight," and so on—are similarly rooted in biblical narrative. As the Canadian literary critic Northrop Frye (1981) emphasized, one cannot grasp the meaning of such expressions without having been exposed, directly or indirectly, to the original biblical stories. These are the source domains for many of the conceptual metaphors we use today for judging human actions and offering advice, bestowing on everyday life an unconscious metaphysical meaning and value. When we say "An eye for an eye and a tooth for a tooth," we are invoking imagery that reverberates with religious meaning in a largely unconscious way.

Science, too, is largely based on metaphorical reasoning. Science often involves things that cannot be seen—atoms, waves, gravitational forces, magnetic fields, and so on. So, scientists use metaphor to get a look, so to speak, at this hidden matter. That is why waves are said to *undulate* through empty space, atoms to *leap* from one quantum state to another, electrons to *travel in circles* around an atomic nucleus, and so forth. As physicist Robert Jones (1982: 4) aptly puts it, for the scientist metaphor serves as "an evocation of the inner connection among things." When a metaphor is accepted as fact, it enters human life, taking on an independent conceptual existence in the real world, suggesting ways to bring about changes in and to the world. Even the nature of experimentation can be seen in this light. Experimentation is a search for connections, linkages, associations of some sort or other. As Rom Harré (1981: 23) has pointed out, most experiments involve "the attempt to relate the structure of things, discovered in an exploratory study, to the organization this imposes on the processes going on in that structure." The physicist K. C. Cole (1984: 156), similarly, puts it as follows:

> The words we use are metaphors; they are models fashioned from familiar ingredients and nurtured with the help of fertile imaginations. "When a physicist says an electron is like a particle", writes physics professor Douglas Giancoli, "he is making a metaphorical comparison like the poet who says "love is like a rose". In both images a concrete object, a rose or a particle, is used to illuminate an abstract idea, love or electron.

Whorf (1956: 213) himself summarized the connection between science and language in this famous quote:

> We dissect nature along lines laid down by our native language. The categories and types that we isolate from the world of phenomena we do not find there because they stare every observer in the face; on the contrary, the world is presented in a kaleidoscope flux of impressions which has to be organized by our minds—and this means largely by the linguistic systems of our minds. We cut nature up, organize it into concepts, and ascribe significances as we do, largely because we are parties to an agreement to organize it in this way—an agreement that holds throughout our speech community and is codified in the patterns of our language, all observers are not led by the same physical evidence to the same picture of the universe, unless their linguistic backgrounds are similar, or can in some way be calibrated.

Returning to Whorf's characterization of figurative language as synesthetic, with which we started off this chapter, consider, again, "The professor is a snake." The choice of the *snake* vehicle produces a mental sensorium—that is, it evokes displaced sensations that relate to how we might react to a real snake. This is a synesthetic effect, which occurs not from individual elements in the expression, but in their relationships to each other. Each linguistic metaphor derived from the *people are animals* concept implies a different synesthetic reaction to it. Portraying *John* as a *monkey*, for instance, impels us to imagine a human person in simian terms. If we were to call *John* a *snake*, a *pig*, or a *puppy*, then our synesthetic image of *John* would change in kind each time—he would become serpentine, swine-like, and puppy-like in our mind's eye.

The Estonian semiotician Yuri Lotman (1991) claimed that culture had figurative structure, which resulted from *energeia*, a kind of "creative potency" that undergirds the invention of words, artistic texts, and all the other expressive-representational products that emanate from it. This *energeia* is likely to be the source of ICM connective structure, allowing people in a specific culture to perceive distinct bits of information and real-world phenomena as connected to each other and to larger frames of meaning metaphorically (again, in cultural terms). The seemingly disparate elements of everyday cultural life thus become unified in the act of figurative connectivity itself.

Epilogue

Whorf himself saw no particular implications in metaphorical language for supporting linguistic relativity, as discussed. But then, as Lakoff (1987) pointed out, Whorf was eccentric. Despite his insightful writings on the connection between language and science, Whorf also seemed to support creationism, writing a lengthy manuscript on the subject in 1925, submitting it to several publishers who promptly rejected it. It is reported that he became rather upset when he sent a briefer manuscript on the topic to an eminent geneticist who answered him with a point-by-point rebuttal of his arguments. So, to understand why he might be wrong, he decided to study Hebrew, so that he could grasp the meanings of the words written in the Bible in one of the original languages of biblical writing. It is not known what became of his creationist views afterwards. The fact that he no longer pursued publication of his creationist ideas is, arguably, indirect evidence that he either abandoned them, or else did not see them as relevant to his larger project of studying language and thought.

Putting aside Whorf's eccentricity, it was Lakoff (1987) who first saw a strong connection between metaphorical language and linguistic relativity, identifying the kinds of questions that this connection elicits:

1. Will studying figurative language reveal the degree and depth of linguistic relativity, in terms of cognitive differences that permeate linguistic and cultural systems?
2. How do conceptual systems evolve?
3. What does the translatability (or not) of metaphor imply in LRH terms?
4. Is the focus of linguistic relativity in language or the brain?

The late writer and social critic Susan Sontag cogently argued, in her compelling 1978 book *Illness as Metaphor*, that the ways in which we speak about a disease predisposes us to think about it in specific ways. The metaphors created and utilized historically to describe a disease may have moral judgments built into them of which we are not consciously aware, thus affecting how the brain understands it. This has a potential psychosomatic effect that affects not only how we think about an illness, but also how we may react to it physically. Using the example of cancer, Sontag suggested that, in the not too distant past, the very word *cancer* would have been more deleterious to a patient's health than some of the actual physiological aspects of the malignancy from which the patient suffered: "As long as a particular disease is treated as an evil, invincible predator, not just a disease, most people with cancer will indeed be demoralized by learning what disease they have" (Sontag 1978: 7). Common examples of how we refer to cancer to this day (in addition to the ones used above) bring out what Sontag was implying:

1. Cancer is a *killer*.
2. Cancer is a *predator*.
3. It's an uphill *battle* to beat cancer.
4. Cancer is a *scourge*.

These metaphors instill the unconscious perception that cancer is an "enemy" that must be defeated, rather than a clinical condition that is serious medically. There are many metaphorical expressions that not only depict cancer as an evil force that has attacked someone, but also as a condition that has been inflicted on someone for moral (or immoral) reasons ("He didn't deserve it;" "She had it coming with their smoking habits;" and so on). Sontag's point that people suffer as much from the judgments about their disease expressed in metaphorical terms than from the disease itself is, indeed, a well-taken and instructive one. A decade after *Illness as Metaphor*, Sontag wrote a similar treatise on AIDS (Sontag 1989), finding a similar pattern of metaphorical evaluation of that disease. Her main point was that illness is not a metaphor, but that we invariably think of diseases in metaphorical ways and these affect the illness to varying degrees in terms of how people react to it.

The number of metaphors that we have created to refer to health and disease is truly mind-boggling, suggesting, as Lakoff and Johnson (1980: 15, 50) have illustrated, that they influence how we perceive health:

1. You're at the *peak* of your health.
2. My health is *down*.
3. You're in *top shape*.
4. My body is *working* perfectly.
5. My body is *breaking down*.
6. My health is *going down* the drain.
7. His pain *went away*.
8. I'm going to *flush out* my cold.

The first three sentences represent health in terms of an orientation metaphor—that is, the state of being healthy is conceptualized as being oriented in an upwards direction, while the opposite state is conceptualized as being oriented in a downwards direction. This is probably due to the fact that, as Lakoff and Johnson (1980: 15) point out, serious "illness forces us to lie down physically." Sentences (4) and (5) show that health and its converse are conceptualized in terms of the metaphorical concept of the *body as a machine*. And, in the last three sentences, health and its converse are envisaged as being entities or substances within a person. This is why they can *go away* and can be *flushed out*. Metaphors have guided medical practices and therapies that envision pain as something that can be detected and eliminated by correcting defects in the machine. This line of thought is traced to Jacques de la Mettrie's 1748 book *L'homme machine*, which describes medical techniques as "repairs" in the biological machinery. Speakers of Tagalog, on the other hand, are inclined to experience disease as intertwined with the overall state of wellbeing of the person, not separate from it.

To conclude this chapter, it should be emphasized that the research in cognitive linguistics has come forth to provide concrete implications for studying the LRH. We hardly ever realize how laden with metaphorical thought everyday speech is—speech that goes back considerably in time. When we talk about an *Achilles' heel* (a weak spot), we are unconsciously taken back to the legend that tells of the mother of the infant Achilles dipping him into the magical river Styx to make him invulnerable. She held him by the heel, however, leaving it unprotected. Achilles was killed subsequently by an arrow to his heel. Similarly, when we speak of a *Herculean task* (tough labor), we are evoking the story of Hercules, the demigod, son of Zeus. Zeus's wife, Hera, was so jealous of Hercules that she set him a dozen impossible tasks to perform, which he nevertheless accomplished, thus becoming immortal. And when we allude to *Pandora's box* to describe something that is unwanted, we are referring to Pandora's curiosity as the source of human misfortune. The gods gave her a box into which each one had put something harmful. They forbade her ever to open it. In time, her curiosity got the better of her and she removed the lid, releasing all evil into the world.

Discussion Questions and Activities

Chapter Questions

1. How is figurative language interconnected with cognition?
2. How does metaphor manifest itself in language and discourse?
3. Does figurative language guide actions and behaviors?

Related Questions

4. What specific aspects of ICM theory are supportive of the LRH? How could these be verified empirically?
5. How would you explain the conceptual differences between metaphor, metonymy, and irony? In what way could they be connected?
6. The following expressions describe *ideas*. How does each one do so? And what does it tell us plausibly about how we understand abstractions?
   (a) Your idea is growing on me.
   (b) Your idea is a square one.
   (c) Your idea is not clear to me.
7. After having read this chapter, do you think that all abstract thought is metaphorical in nature or origin, or not? Explain, illustrate, and defend your point of view.
8. Do you think that knowledge is forged by metaphor? Defend your position.

Activities

1. Below are a few of the ways in which *love* is expressed in English. On which conceptual metaphor is each one based? For example, "We went on a honeymoon" is derived from the conceptual metaphor, *love is a sweet taste*.
   (a) Our relationship is on hold.
   (b) We cannot keep going like this; we must either turn back or abandon the relationship altogether.
   (c) We're spinning our wheels.
   (d) Our relationship is off the track.
   (e) It is on the rocks.
2. Two common image schemata in English are:
   (a) The *impediment* image schema ("You must get over your troubles;" "She could not be stopped by her troubles;" etc.)
   (b) The *journey* image schema ("Our society has come a long way in civil rights legislation;" "We cannot allow this to fall by the wayside;" etc.).
   Apply these to the following concepts: for example, if you are given the concept of *success*, a relevant instantiation of the *impediment* image schema could be, "Nothing will stop me from succeeding;" a relevant instantiation of the *journey* schema could be, "You have a long way to go before becoming the CEO of that company."
   (a) friendship
   (b) justice

(c) hope
(d) jealousy
(e) ambition.
3. Give examples of anthropomorphism in English pertaining to the following concepts: for example, if given *storm*, a relevant example would be *eye of the storm*.
   (a) wind
   (b) mountain
   (c) journey
   (d) computers
   (e) automobiles.
4. What conceptual metaphor does each expression reveal? What could each one tell us about the perception of things?
   (a) He's a lightning rod.
   (b) Your friend is a real fox.
   (c) My house is a hole.
   (d) My computer is a treasure.
   (e) My life is hell.
5. Draw up your own ICMs for *love* and *thinking*, comparing the source domains for each, indicating whether clustering or radiative connectivity is involved. Then draw up ICMs for the two concepts in any other language you know. Compare them with the corresponding English ICMs.

7
COMPUTER-MEDIATED COMMUNICATION, AI, AND ARTIFICIAL LANGUAGES

Prologue

The age of the computer and the Internet has changed many rules regarding how we communicate and use language. The study of computer-mediated communication (CMC), as it is called, has many potential implications for examining linguistic relativity, presenting us with a picture of how languages evolve in mediated environments and how the resulting changes in linguistic forms may affect changes in thought. Studies of CMC are showing, for instance, that it has an effect on impression formation, on the dynamics of person-to-person and group-to-group interaction, on inhibition factors, and other social-emotional aspects of communication (Greenfield 2015). In effect, CMC provides a new field laboratory for testing out various aspects of the LRH.

Also relevant to the study of the LRH in today's world is the work on language comprehension and production in artificial intelligence (AI). Can human thought be modeled in computer software in any verisimilar way? Can a computer ever *understand* language as humans do? If so, what would that truly mean? These questions have received relatively little attention by Whorfian-based research; but they are clearly relevant to it. On the other side, if AI researchers expect to create machines that think like humans, they will have to take the Whorfian perspective seriously into account, for it provides specific insights into how we think *with* and *through* language—that is, how the categories of a language shape cognitive or perceptual mechanisms, how they are connected to worldviews, and so on. In other words, AI researchers will need to ensure that an AI system can carry out such cognitive tasks as the ability to "talk to itself"—a key feature of natural cognition, as Vygotsky so insightfully showed in his study of linguistic development in children (Chapter 2). This chapter will discuss some of the Whorfian implications connected to both CMC and AI. General conclusions with regard to the LRH will be summarized at the end.

The questions that will inform the discussion in this chapter are the following:

1. What implications can be extracted for assessing the LRH from studying CMC?
2. What can work in AI tell us about the validity (or invalidity) of the LRH?
3. What implications can be gleaned from studying artificial languages?

Computer-Mediated Communication

CMC is communication that occurs through the use of electronic devices. Facebook, Twitter, text-messaging, posting, sharing links, and so on all constitute digital conversational spaces based on CMC, which can be synchronous and asynchronous. The latter occurs when interlocutors are not necessarily aware that a message has occurred until they are informed about it through some electronic signal—this characterizes emails, bulletin boards, blogs, chatrooms, etc. Synchronous CMC occurs, instead, when the interlocutor is aware of the communication as an ongoing one, as in back-and-forth text-messaging. CMC has had implications for various branches of linguistics. One is the study of *speech networks*, which are groups of speakers united through virtual spaces, rather than geographical ones, and thus classified according to frequency of interaction and the strength of the contact. People in "dense networks" have frequent (daily) contact with each other, and are thus likely to be linked by more than one type of bond than are those with infrequent contact, forming "weak networks." Dense networks put pressure on members to conform because their values can be more readily shared.

As E. Gabriella Coleman (2010: 488) has aptly put it, "digital artifacts have helped engender new collectivities." She argues that these have had a significant impact on everyday life:

> Digital media feed into, reflect, and shape other kinds of social practices, like economic exchange, financial markets, and religious worship. Attention to these rituals, broad contexts, and the material infrastructures and social protocols that enable them illuminates how the use and production of digital media have become integrated into everyday cultural, linguistic, and economic life.

Her observation can be interpreted in Whorfian terms as follows: language adapts to new digital media and this adaptation affects the nexus between language, thought, and discourse. One area of particular relevance to studying this nexus is what British linguist David Crystal (2006) has called *netlingo* to describe the compressed forms of language used in text messages, social networking sites, and the like. Netlingo is marked by efficiency of structure, which manifests itself in such phenomena as abbreviations, acronyms, and alphanumeric symbols, all of which are designed to make the delivery of linguistic messages rapid and highly economical: *b4* = *before*, *bf/gf* = *boyfriend/girlfriend*, *lol* = *laugh out loud*, and so on. Now, do these compressed forms entail a shift on how we understand messages? Does compression of form affect thought? It is relevant to note that abbreviated writing has always been used for reasons of efficiency by scholars, scientists, and various official agencies. Forms such as *etc.*, *ibid.*, *laser*, and even *radio* come from the fields of scholarship and science. And abbreviated or acronymic forms—such as *UNESCO*, *TGIF*, *ad*, *TV*, and the like—predate netlingo. Some social critics, such as Mark Helprin (2009), caution that the new forms of CMC are not convenient abbreviations, but rather new forms of language that produce an addictive effect on people and how they process information, rendering people much less reflective and less inclined to appreciate literary greatness. Others respond that it is no more than an efficient way to create written messages for informal communication in digital spaces. People use it not to generate thoughtfulness and literary communication but, rather, to keep in contact and to facilitate communication. In no way does this imply that people have lost the desire to read and reflect on the world. Netlingo is not a revolutionary development in linguistic communication; it is an evolutionary-adaptive one, having emerged to increase the speed at which messages can be inputted and read.

A relevant aspect of CMC is its multimodality, allowing for visual symbols, such as emojis, to be used in tandem with textual writing. Alphabetic writing involves knowledge of phonemics, grammatical structure, and vocabulary choices. An emoji text does not—it is visual, not phonemic. Thus, it is presumably more broadly understandable than a message written in some specific language, since it does not require competence in that language. Emojis raise a whole set of Whorfian questions. For instance: To what part of speech will an emoji be assigned psychologically? A cloud emoji, for instance, is likely to be perceived as a noun corresponding to the word *cloud*. A sunrise emoji, on the other hand, showing the shape of a sun as it rises up from a background, suggests either the noun *sunrise*, or a verb describing the *rising* of the sun. Now, these very same emoji forms could be used to describe something (such as a *cloudy mood* or a *sunny disposition*), thus functioning also as metaphorical adjectives. In a cloud emoji, the grayish-white color can also be used in messages to suggest various emotions (such as dullness or boredom); the sunrise emoji may suggest an uplifting of emotions or something similar. In effect, it is difficult to assign emojis to specific parts of speech, because they are conceptually multifunctional. Some linguists see emojis as part of a visual gesture language replacing the actual gestures, facial expressions, and so on of face-to-face communication (Evans 2017). This seems plausible but here, too, it is difficult to discern how these would fit into a system of replacement-communication. Clearly, CMC is an open area of research that begs many theoretical questions.

The initial objective of Unicode, the originator of current emojis, was to enhance communication among everyone in the global village, despite different languages, believing that the emoji code would constitute a kind of visual Esperanto understandable across cultures in approximately the same ways. In other words, emojis were designed artificially as a universal visual *lingua franca* but, over time, this has turned out to be impracticable, as users from different language backgrounds have ended up interpreting them in terms of culture-specific meanings. In effect, emojis are hardly perceived universally as pictures of the same emotions, gestures, or whatever else they are designed to be; rather, they produce semiotic relativity effects (Danesi 2016b) that vary according to users of specific languages. For example, even the smiley figure—which was meant to be as culturally neutral as possible, having been designed as a simple facial circle colored in yellow as an obvious attempt to remove recognizable facial features associated with race or ethnicity—has created relativity effects. Almost immediately after it spread into universal usage, it became subject to culturally shaped meanings, leading to new designs, including shades of color. The result has been an attenuation of the desired universality of the code and, consequently, of the universality of the purported universal principles of communication it was meant to subserve.

A subtext in the emoji movement recalls the idea that a universal form of communication would lead to a collectivity of mind, constituting what Peter Russell (1983) called a *global brain*. Global Brain Theory claims that our brains are shaped by the environment in which we live and which we ourselves make. With a new communication system, such as the emoji code, our brains can presumably be rewired. In this paradigm, intelligence is collective or distributed, not centralized in any particular person, institution, or system. This means that no one individual can control it; the system organizes itself—called emergence—from the networks and processes of interaction between the components. Implications for the LRH are obvious: Is the groupthink of the global brain different from individual-think of individual brains? Does emoji writing, which is pictorial, encourage groupthink or not? Research forays into these questions remain, at present, largely untraveled.

Artificial Intelligence

An intriguing area of research, with implications for the LRH, is the modeling of language on computer programs, an area that connects linguistics with AI research (Guzman 2018). The questions that such research elicits are significant ones for testing the language–thought nexus. We can recreate language, but can we recreate the complex thought patterns that it reflects or shapes? If we could, it would mean that the computer will develop consciousness, with the ability to talk to itself and to think about itself. Is this plausible? Could there be human–machine communication (HMC) that is meaningful beyond the exchange of information, instructions, and the like, which are superficial denotative matters of language design?

One of the first experiments in HMC was the Eliza Project, which is worthwhile revisiting briefly here. The project was the idea of Joseph Weizenbaum in 1966. He designed his computer program to mimic the speech that a psychotherapist would use. Eliza's questions—such as "Why do you say your head hurts?" in response to "My head hurts"—were perceived by subjects as being so realistic that many believed that the machine was actually alive. But, as Weizenbaum wrote a decade later, Eliza was a parodic imitation of psychoanalytic therapy speech; it had no consciousness of what it was saying. Weizenbaum's project gave momentum to natural language programming (NLP), with the goal of producing human speech that verged on verisimilitude. Today, NLP uses sophisticated logical, probabilistic, and neural network systems that can produce and comprehend conversations (whatever that means in natural intelligence terms). The probabilistic aspect of NLP is a central one, given that many aspects of human communication involve uncertainty. In this framework, a prior hypothesis is updated in the light of new relevant observations or evidence, and this is done via a set of algorithmic procedures. But the problem of understanding comes up: What would a communication between a human and a machine truly mean? Again, this is an ongoing area of research which is beginning to provide interesting insights, but not any practical results as of yet (to the best of my knowledge).

NLP programs are quite sophisticated; for instance, they can determine the sense of, say, an ambiguous word on the basis of word collocations in a text. A collocation is a sequence of words that typically co-occur in speech more often than would be anticipated by random chance. Collocations are not idioms, which have fixed phraseology. Phrases such as *crystal clear*, *cosmetic surgery*, and *clean bill of health* are all collocations. Whether the collocation is derived from some syntactic (*make choices*) or lexical (*clear-cut*) criterion, the principle underlying collocations—frequency of usage of words in tandem—always applies. And it is this principle that undergirds predictive NLP algorithms. But the correct choice of a word is a statistical option, not an option based on experience and inner savvy. Moreover, collocations, and many other such formulaic phrases, are based on figurative language. And this fact has stimulated interest among computer scientists: Is metaphor programmable? Among the first to model metaphorical expressions computationally were Eric MacCormac (1985) and James M. Martin (1990), who were able easily to model so-called "frozen metaphors," those that have lost their metaphorical meanings due to frequency of usage, judiciously omitting the computational study of creative or novel metaphors—which, as they admitted, were virtually impossible to model (at the time). An example of a frozen metaphor is "I see your point," which is based on the conceptual metaphor *ideas are geometrical figures*, whereby *point* is no longer sensed to have metaphorical meaning. Because of its data-processing and data-mining capacities, a computer can examine a corpus for metaphoricity such as this in real speech, but it will not know what a new metaphor means, unless it is reprogrammed into the computer's algorithms—that is, the computer can produce new metaphorical language, but it takes a human brain to interpret it first.

The review of the relevant literature by Holyoak and Stamenkovic (2018) has identified the kind of research in the field that needs to be conducted in order to truly model metaphor comprehension:

1. Distinguishing algorithmically between conceptual and linguistic metaphor
2. Distinguishing between frozen and novel metaphors
3. Defining multiword metaphorical expressions
4. Programming extended metaphor and metaphor in discourse.

Currently, there is no way to program into a computer the same kinds of associative structures that guide human metaphorical cognition, or that respond to the relativity effects that these produce in speakers of languages. Actually, early work by Kenneth E. Iverson (1962, 1980) suggested that the programming language itself had relativity effects, since, as Iverson claimed, the more powerful the notions and symbols used in computer algorithms, the more they aided human thinking. Similarly, Paul Graham (2010) has examined how computer languages produced effects on conceptualization. He called the effects the *Blub Paradox*, which says that anyone who prefers a certain programming language will *know* how powerful it is because *writing* in the language means *thinking* in it; hence the paradox that programmers are "satisfied with whatever language they happen to use, because it dictates the way they think about programs."

In sum, the main problems that AI must resolve involve meaning. Humans use language with a host of meaning-making functions, from a simple description of events ("The cat is on the mat") to interpretation

("The cat is very friendly") and imagination ("Cats are clever creatures"). The closer to denotative information content (such as in descriptive language), the easier it is for AI to produce viable results. The other functions (interpretation and imagination) are likely to remain exclusive to human brains. Moreover, the concept of consciousness of identity associated with the language one speaks is a problematic one for AI to resolve. Someone who is reared in a French-speaking environment will grow to be a "French person," having acquired all the meanings of that language. If the same person were reared in a Russian-speaking environment, the individual would instead grow to be a "Russian person," with all the values and meanings inscribed in that language. What would this mean in AI terms?

In his 2005 book *The Singularity is Near*, Ray Kurzweil maintains that there will come a moment in time when AI will have progressed to a point that it will autonomously outperform human intelligence. That moment, known as the *Technological Singularity*, will occur when an upgradable software becomes self-sufficient without human intervention, thus becoming capable of self-improvements (Kurzweil 1999, 2012). This term was introduced by science fiction writer Vernor Vinge in his 1980 story "The Names." He followed this up with a 1993 article titled "The Coming Technological Singularity," in which he maintained that his fictional vision would become a reality in the first part of the twenty-first century. Actually, the whole idea can be traced back to a comment made by mathematician John van Neumann, cited by Stanislas Ulam (1958: 5): "[The] ever accelerating progress of technology and changes in the mode of human life, which gives the appearance of approaching some essential singularity in the history of the race beyond which human affairs, as we know them, could not continue." The research in this domain of AI is now called *Seed AI*; it seeks to create machines that are capable of improving their own software and hardware by rewriting their own source code without human intervention.

The Singularity implies that, at a certain point, AI will become conscious of what it is doing (Bor 2012). But the word *consciousness* is meaningless without human definition. So, to avoid this ambiguity, Kurzweil (1999) has used the designation "mind-beyond-machine," which alludes to the original Cartesian view that the mind is a machine that is activated by some animal spirit. The difference in Singularity theory is that the animal spirit is replaced by algorithms. But this raises a host of questions: Will AI be capable of seemingly specific human traits, such as humor and irony? Can it create new meanings on the basis of new experiences? To do these, AI would have to reverse-engineer the human brain—an area that is actually receiving serious attention under the rubric of Artificial General Intelligence (AGI) (Hawkins and Blakeslee 2004)—which, if realizable, would likely produce machines that imitate neural functions, rather than reproduce them in any human way. Several projects have been initiated to carry out reverse-engineering using quantum computers, which need not concern us here. The human mind and body are interactive agents in the production of cognitive structures—that is, human thought is shaped by aspects of the body beyond perception and cognition, and it is embedded in relevant linguistic categories.

Artificial Languages

Creating artificial languages that could enable new, and perhaps better, ways of thinking has been a goal that goes back in time considerably. The premise is that, by eliminating all the biases and prejudices that natural languages make available, we could create a utopia where language is always honest and straightforward, being as culturally neutral as possible (Okrent 2009). Examples of artificial languages designed to explore the human mind include Loglan, explicitly designed by James Cooke Brown (1960) to test the LRH, by using it to investigate whether it would make its speakers think more logically, rather than emotionally or prejudicially. As far as can be told, experimental uses of Loglan to test this hypothesis have been inconclusive. Similar attempts to create culturally neutral artificial languages include: Láadan, by Suzette Haden Elgin (see Elgin and Martin 1988), which, she claimed, made it easier to express the "female worldview," as opposed to SAE languages which she considered to be based on a "male centered" worldview; Ithkuil by John Quijada, designed to get speakers to become consciously aware of the categories they are using in speech (see Quijada 2011); and Toki Pona, by Sonja Lang, a language based on Taoist philosophy that she hopes would steer human thought towards the holistic Taoist worldview, which is quite similar to the Hopi one in many ways (see Lang 2014). As far as can be told, none of these has been examined empirically from the standpoint of the LRH—a research paradigm that would allow for testing out such premises as the connection between cognition, perception, and memory to a language that did not emerge from a historical cultural context.

The idea of a perfect language goes back to the story of the Tower of Babel. More than 200 artificial languages have been invented across time. A seventeenth-century clergyman, John Wilkins, wrote an essay in which he proposed a language in which words would be built to bear universal meanings. Volapük—invented in 1879 by Johann Martin Schleyer, a German priest—was the earliest of these languages to gain moderate currency. The name of the language comes from two of its words meaning "world" and "speak." Today, only Esperanto is used somewhat and studied as an indirect theory of the language-thought nexus. It was invented by Polish physician Ludwik Lejzer Zamenhof. The name is derived from the pen name Zamenhof used, Dr. Esperanto. The word *Esperanto* means, as Zamenhof explained it, "one who hopes." Esperanto has a simple morphological structure—adjectives end in /-a/, adverbs end in /-e/, nouns end in /-o/, /-n/ is added at the end of a noun used as an object, and plural forms end in /-j/. The core vocabulary of Esperanto consists mainly of root morphemes common to the Indo-European languages. The following sentence is written in Esperanto: *La astronauto, per speciala instrumento, fotografas la lunon* = "The astronaut, with a special instrument, photographs the moon."

Esperanto espouses the goal of standardizing language so that ideas can be communicated in the same way across cultures. Some estimates peg the number of speakers of Esperanto today from 100,000 to over one million. It is difficult to quantify the number of speakers accurately, as there is no specific territory or nation that uses the language. Zamenhof actually did not want Esperanto to replace native or indigenous languages; he intended it as a universal *second* language, providing a common linguistic vehicle for communication among people from different linguistic backgrounds. The Universala Esperanto-Asocio (Universal Esperanto Association), founded in 1908, has chapters in over 100 countries. Cuba has radio broadcasts in Esperanto. There are a number of periodicals published in Esperanto, including *Monato*, a news magazine published in Belgium. Some novelists, such as the Hungarian author Julio Baghy and the French author Raymond Schwartz, have written works in Esperanto.

It is ironic to note, however, that research on Esperanto indicates that it has a tendency to develop dialects, and that it is undergoing various predictable changes (diachronically speaking), thus impugning its *raison d'être*. Benjamin Bergen (2001) discovered that, even in the first generation of speakers, Esperanto had undergone considerable changes in its morphology and that it had borrowed words from other languages. So, perfect languages may not be possible after all, either as devised by computers or humans. The structure of grammar and vocabulary in computer and artificial languages is reduced to a bare outline of natural language grammar and vocabulary, and meaning is generally restricted to a denotative range— one-word-one-meaning. In a phrase, the idea is to eliminate culture-specific knowledge networks from human language.

There have, of course, been actual languages used in the international arena for purposes of global communication. One such language in Europe was Latin, which, for centuries during the medieval and Renaissance periods, was used by theologians, scholars, and scientists to communicate among themselves across Europe. It was also the official language of the Church. A little later, French took its place, called appropriately a *lingua franca*. Today, the *lingua franca* would seem to be English (and should thus be called more accurately a *lingua anglica*), given its prevalence in Internet communications, not to mention in international forums, such as scientific conferences. But the use of the language of any one particular society is fraught with a whole series of problems, into which we cannot go here. Suffice it to say that the nonnative users of the *lingua anglica* would probably not be using the linguistic resources of English in a conceptually appropriate fashion, thus leading to misunderstanding—which is precisely what is not intended.

Artificial languages are not the only "made-up" languages that have interesting features in them for linguists to examine. There are, for example, languages made up by writers, such as the languages of Quenya and Sindarin, found in J. R. Tolkein's *The Lord of the Rings* series of books, and the Klingon language in the *Star Trek* series of TV programs and movies. These languages are interesting because they show, above all else, that natural languages leave conceptual gaps, offering up only a portion of what is potentially knowable in the world. Indeed, an infinite number of words and expressions could be created without any meanings attached to them. This is exactly what young children do when they make up nonsense words, creating them seemingly only for the pleasure of making imitative, pleasant, or humorous sound effects.

Epilogue

The questions that have guided the discussion in this chapter include what can be gleaned about the LRH by examining CMC, computer languages, computer models of language, and artificially constructed languages. Can a computer have the same *thoughts* as a human by using language? Would the machine *know* what it is thinking? The argument that this is unlikely was made a while back by John Searle (1984), who made the case that computers cannot think in the way humans can. Searle argued that a computer does not know what it is doing when it processes symbols, because it lacks intentionality. Just like an English-speaking human being who translates Chinese symbols in the form of little pieces of paper by using a set of rules for matching them with other symbols, or little pieces of paper, knows nothing about the "story" contained in the Chinese pieces of paper, a computer does not have access to the "story" inhering in human symbols.

Language is hardly an information-processing device; it is an interpretive system, transforming input from the world into categories of language and symbolism. This system was called the *Bauplan* by the biologist Jakob von Uexküll at the turn of the twentieth century (1909). Von Uexküll established a point of contact between the mainstream scientific approach to the study of organisms, biology, and that of the field of semiotics. For von Uexküll, every organism had different inward and outward "lives." The key to understanding this duality was in the anatomical structure of the organism itself. Animals with widely divergent anatomies do not live in the same kind of world. There exists, therefore, no common world of objects shared by humans and animals equally. The work of von Uexküll has shown that an organism does not perceive an object in itself, but according to its own particular kind of *Bauplan*—the pre-existent mental modeling system that allows it to interpret the world of beings, objects, and events in a biologically determined way. For von Uexküll, this system is grounded in the organism's body, which routinely converts the external world of experience into an internal one of representation in terms of the particular features of the *Bauplan* with which a specific species is endowed.

The *Bauplan* of AI and artificial languages is hardly designed to interpret input in the same way as humans, but, rather, to algorithmicize it. Mathematician and computer scientist Norbert Wiener (1948) established a science to study how self-contained complex systems are analogous, calling it "cybernetics." The science is not interested in the material forms of the systems but, instead, in the ways in which the forms are organized to constitute the systems. Because of the increasing sophistication of computers and the efforts to make them behave in human-like ways, cybernetics today is closely allied with AI and robotics, also drawing on ideas developed in information theory. Wiener developed cybernetics from observing that people, nonhuman animals, and machines carried out their functions in purposeful and orderly ways, seeking stability in the enactment of these methods. One of the most important shared characteristics was feedback, which involves the circling back of information to a control device (such as the human brain) to adjust behavior or functioning. For instance, when a human being's body temperature is too high or too low, the body feeds this information back to the brain. The brain then reacts to correct the temperature, or to suggest ways to seek a solution. A household thermostat functions in much the same way, using feedback to adjust the operation of a furnace to maintain a fixed temperature. Some argue that cybernetics started a second revolution, called the "information society," a revolution that has displaced the previous Industrial Age. Whatever the case, it is clear that the work in cybernetics will be of relevance to studying the LRH: What can we learn from the languages that crystallize naturally in computer simulations, or those constructed as substitutes for existing languages?

Implications of Linguistic Relativity

To conclude this textbook, it is useful to go over a few of its main themes. First, the whole line of research on linguistic relativity should not be centered exclusively on the language–mind nexus but, rather, on a broader range of human sign use—a perspective called "semiotic relativity." In most discussions and debates surrounding the LRH there is little space given to the imagination as a likely precursor of thinking, which implies that thought can emerge initially without language, as a means of grasping the world intuitively. This form of imaginative thinking is translated by the *Bauplan* into language forms that subsequently allow humans to explore the imagined thoughts. So, what Whorfian researchers have called "thinking before speaking" should be modified to "imagining before thinking and speaking." Of course, one would have to consider what is meant by the term *imagination*, which is problematic. That said, it could actually be that, by examining how creative language, such as metaphor, emerges, we can get a glimpse into what is involved in imaginative cognition.

The LRH is an important idea for linguistics, semiotics, anthropology, psychology, computer science, and other disciplines involved in studying the human mind. As Wolff and Holmes (2011) have perceptively outlined, there are various aspects that the LRH evokes that have been debated and researched since it became intrinsic to linguistic anthropology and psychology:

1. Thought is language (strong version).
2. Language affects thought (weak version).
3. Thought is separate from language (universalism).
4. Thought and language are structurally parallel.
5. Thought and language differ structurally.
6. Thought occurs with language, but may also occur after language.

These can be integrated into an overall model expressed by the notion of the Whorfian Scale, which suggests that there are some aspects that indicate that thought is separate from language, and these would fall near the 0 point on the scale; there are, instead, aspects that tie thought to the native vocabulary and grammar, and these would fall near the 1 point on the scale. All others can be seen to fall in between these two points. Also, as discussed in this chapter the language–thought nexus requires another dimension to it—its adaptation to new media. Language, mind, and media are thus variables in a single equation—when one of these changes in the equation so, too, do the others. Sometimes the trigger for change may be the language itself; at other times it may be the medium; and at yet other times it may be new social thoughts that appear from various associative and cognitive processes on their own.

The LRH has many social and cognitive implications—it has been used to explain sexism, racism, and even so-called *hypocognition*, which refers to the inability to communicate certain ideas because there are no words for them (Levy 1973; Hollan 2000). The term was coined by Robert Levy (1973) after conducting ethnographic research among native Tahitians, finding that they had no words to describe sorrow or guilt, instead referring to sadness as feeling sick or strange, which he believed contributed to their high depression rate. George Lakoff used it to describe political progressives in the United States, saying that, relative to conservatives, they suffer from "massive hypocognition" (Lakoff 2004: 54). Hypocognition has been blamed for preventing the use of evidence-based medicine and for leading to negative consequences in other areas of social behavior, where words are lacking (Mariotto 2010; Wu and Dunning 2018). Clearly, the study of the LRH is not just a whim for linguists; it is critical for understanding human actions and behaviors—at least, in principle.

Concluding Remarks

During Euclid's time, and for centuries thereafter, the worldview of philosophers, scientists, and mathematicians was shaped by his ideas. One of his axioms, which seemed to be perfectly logical and "evident," was the so-called parallel postulate:

> If a straight line crossing two straight lines makes the interior angles on the same side less than two right angles, the two straight lines, if extended indefinitely, meet on that side on which are the angles less than the two right angles.

The gist of the postulate is that two parallel lines will never cross, no matter how infinitely long we make them. The problem was that it was not really a postulate or an axiom, which was demonstrated by mathematicians in the 1800s. This led to the creation of geometric systems in which it was replaced by other postulates. From this, non-Euclidean geometries emerged. In one of these, called "hyperbolic" or "Lobachevskyan" geometry (after Nikolai Lobachevsky), the parallel postulate is replaced by the following: through a point not on a given line, more than one line may be drawn parallel to the given line. In one model of hyperbolic geometry, the plane is defined as a set of points that lie in the interior of a circle. And parallel lines are defined as lines that never intersect. In around 1860, Bernard Riemann had another hunch: Is there a world where no lines are parallel? The practical answer is the surface of a sphere, on which all straight lines are great circles.

Now, the advent of non-Euclidean geometries led, literally, to a new view of space and, ultimately, to a new physics. In other words, they produced semiotic relativity effects, as they have been called here, which led to paradigm shifts in worldview (Kuhn 1970). Language is the primary semiotic means we have for encoding ideas and for reinforcing, spreading, and preserving them. So, geometries must be explained in language, not in lieu of it. One could hardly ever understand a geometric idea that is not explainable linguistically—we would only see figures, lines, etc. without meaning. Language allows us to interpret the world. When the world changes, so too does language—one entails the other. But this presents a paradox. As quantum physicists found out at the start of the twentieth century, since theories are formulated with language, it is unlikely that the truth about the universe will ever be known, because a language can only give us a partial glimpse of reality, selected by the categories of that language. Sometimes these clash. People think of a particle, such as a photon or an electron, as occupying space at a certain point in time, and traveling along a specific path. As it turns out, however, a particle does not really exist until it interacts with something, and it travels down not one path but simultaneously down all possible paths. However, once discovered, the resources of language can be used literally to envision it—hence the term *wavicle*, coined to describe the wave–particle duality concept in quantum mechanics that every particle may be described as either a particle or a wave.

In the end, the connection between thought and language will remain a mystery, as Whorf himself stated (Whorf 1956: 252):

> Thinking is most mysterious, and by far the greatest light upon it that we have is thrown by the study of language. This study shows that the forms of a person's thoughts are controlled by inexorable laws of pattern of which he is unconscious. These patterns are the unperceived intricate systematizations of his own language—shown readily enough by a candid comparison and contrast with other languages, especially those of a different linguistic family. His thinking itself is in a language—in English, in Sanskrit, in Chinese. And every language is a vast pattern-system, different from others, in which are culturally ordained the forms and categories by which the personality not only communicates, but also analyzes nature, notices or neglects types of relationship and phenomena, channels his reasoning, and builds the house of his consciousness.

Discussion Questions and Activities

Chapter Questions

1. What implications can be extracted for assessing the LRH from studying CMC?
2. What can work in AI tell us about the validity (or invalidity) of the LRH?
3. What implications can be gleaned from studying artificial languages?

Related Questions

4. Do you think the Technological Singularity will actually come about? If so, in what ways would AI supersede human intelligence? How would humans adapt?
5. What is the difference between information-processing and interpretation? How relevant is this to the study of the LRH?
6. What is the difference between linguistic relativity and semiotic relativity?
7. Do you think that the native language a scientist speaks may influence the way the scientist interprets data? If so, how so?
8. How do scientists get around the limitations of their specific language?

Activities

1. How would you explain the following in terms of the LRH?
   (a) the meaning of a word
   (b) the meaning of a conversation
   (c) the meaning of a piece of music
   (d) the meaning of a painting
   (e) the meaning of a movie.
   Do you think a computer can be programmed to provide similar meanings? If so, how so? If not, why not?
2. Consider the following netlingo forms. What do you think they mean? Do they bear connotations that differ from their complete versions? For instance, is *lol* different in meaning than *laugh out loud?*
   (a) brb
   (b) btw
   (c) lmk
   (d) g2g
   (e) ilu
   (f) imo
   (g) irl
   (h) yolo.
3. Make a list of the ten commonly-used emojis in English and compare them to their meanings and uses in any other language you know. How would you explain the differences, if any?
4. What kinds of information and meaning would have to be programmed into a computer to mimic or control the following features of human language?
   (a) sound symbolism
   (b) ICMs

(c) irony
(d) polysemy.
5. Go through a dictionary of a language other than English. Set up the following categories of vocabulary, translating them and comparing them to English. What patterns, if any, do you notice? Then, what kind of instructions would be needed to program them into a computer?
   (a) spatial terms
   (b) motion terms
   (c) color terms
   (d) kinship terms.

GLOSSARY

agglutinative language language characterized, in general, by words made up of more than one morpheme (one word = several morphemes): the Turkish word *evlerinizden* ("from your houses") consists of the morphemes /ev-ler-iniz-den/ meaning, respectively, "house-plural-your-from"

analytic language language that depends mainly on word-order to convey meaning (one morpheme = one meaning)

blending theory (conceptual blending theory) theory that language forms result from the blending of various regions in the brain into a distinct concept.

bound morpheme morpheme that is attached to another morpheme: /un-/ and /-ly/ in *unlikely*

calque word-by-word translation of a foreign phrase or expression: the title *The Brothers Karamazov* is a calque of the corresponding Russian phrase (the word order in English should be *The Karamazov Brothers*)

codability the notion that languages encode those concepts that they need

code-switching alternating between two or more languages, or varieties of language in conversation; typical speech characteristic of bilinguals

communicative competence ability to use a language appropriately in social contexts

conceptual metaphor generalized metaphorical formula: *people are animals* underlies *he's a dog*, *she's a tiger*, etc.

connotation extensional meaning of a word: the meaning of *house* as a legislative quorum: *The house is in session* is an example of connotation

context psychological, social, and emotional relations or situations that constrain the type of language used during communication

core vocabulary basic vocabulary of a language, containing items such as *mother, father, son, daughter*, etc.

denotation basic or literal meaning of a word: the meaning of "small feline mammal" for *cat*

derivational morpheme morpheme that is derived from some other morpheme: *happiness* is derived from *happy*

diachronic analysis analysis of change in language

discourse use of language in socially coded or socially relevant ways

distinctive feature minimal trait in a form that serves to keep it distinct from other forms

diversification process of languages developing from a single root

ethnography method of collecting data by living among the subject group and interacting with the group in some direct way

ethnology alternative for *ethnography*

fieldwork research whereby the analyst lives among the subjects

free morpheme morpheme that can exist on its own: *cautious* in *cautiously*

function word word such as *the* or *and* that has grammatical function

generative grammar analysis of language based on examining the types of rules and rule-making principles by which sentences are generated

gesticulant gesture that accompanies vocal speech

gesture communication involving hand movement

grammar system of rules for the formation of words and sentences

ground meaning of a metaphor

idealized cognitive model (ICM) amalgam of source domains used to deliver a cultural concept

innatism view that we are born with a blueprint for language

inner speech thinking with language

intertextuality allusion to texts that are relevant to a language during discourse: for example, allusion to biblical themes in English discourse.

irony word or statement used in such a way that it means the opposite of what it denotes: *What a beautiful day!* uttered on a stormy day

isolating language language that forms its words primarily with single morphemes (one morpheme = one word)

langue theoretical knowledge of a language (its rules, its structure, etc.)

lexeme morpheme with lexical meaning: *logic* in *logical*

lexical field collection of lexemes that are interrelated thematically, such as sports vocabulary

lexicon set of morphemes in a language

linguistic competence abstract knowledge of a language

linguistic performance knowledge of how to use a language

linguistic relativity hypothesis view that languages influence how people come to perceive the world

marked category form that is specific and not representative of an entire category

markedness theory that certain forms in language are basic and that others are derived from them

metaphor process by which something abstract is rendered understandable by reference to something concrete: *love is sweet*

metaphoric gesture gesture accompanying speech that represents the vehicle (concrete part) of a metaphor used in the utterance

metonymy process whereby the part stands for the whole: *the White House* for "the American government"

morpheme minimal unit of meaning: in *cautiously* there are two morphemes *cautious* and *-ly*

morphology level of language where words are formed

netlingo online language with its particular compressed forms and other peculiarities

opposition difference that keeps units distinct, such as the opposition between *night* and *day*

parameter feature of a specific language that manifests a more general innate principle

parole knowledge of how to use a language

phatic communion formulaic speech designed for bonding and social contact purposes

phoneme minimal unit of sound that distinguishes meaning

phonetics description of how sounds are articulated

phonology sound system of a language

polysemy the various meanings of a word: such as *affair*, which can mean a "business transaction," "a romantic tryst," etc.

poverty of the stimulus notion that children must already know a great deal about language since they start talking simply by being exposed to partial and imperfect input

pragmatics study of discourse

prefix affix that is added before another morpheme: the *il-* in *illogical*

prototypical concept basic member of a category: *cat* is a prototypical member of the *feline* category

referent what a word refers to

relativity effects effects produced on thinking by a language

semantics study of meaning in language

semiotic relativity view that all sign systems participate in shaping thought—verbal and nonverbal

sign something that stands for something other than itself

sound symbolism use of sounds to construct words in such a way that they resemble the sound properties of their referents, or to bring out some sound-based perception of meaning: *crash* stands for the actual sound to which it refers

source domain concrete part of a conceptual metaphor: the *sweet* in *love is sweet*

specialized vocabulary vocabulary used to describe specific things: color terms, seating devices, etc.

speech act specific use of language to imply an action

subordinate concept concept that provides detail: for example, *Siamese* details a type of cat

suffix affix added to the end of a morpheme: *-ly* in *logically*

superordinate concept general concept: *animal*, rather than *cat*

synchronic analysis study of language at a particular point in time, usually the present

synecdoche concept in which the part represents the whole: *head* in *head of the organization*

syntax study of how phrases, clauses, sentences, and entire texts are organized

synthetic language highly inflectional language that does not depend on word order

target domain topic of a conceptual metaphor: *love* in *love is sweet*

tenor topic of a metaphor: *professor* in *the professor is a sweetheart*

topic what the metaphor is about: the *love* in *love is sweet*

typological classification classifying languages according to the type of grammatical system they have

universal grammar set of rule-making principles present in the brain at birth that make up the language faculty

unmarked category default form in a class of forms

vehicle concrete part of a metaphor: the *sweet* in *love is sweet*

vocabulary set of morphemes in a language, or in some discourse, conversation, etc.

Whorfian Hypothesis theory which posits that a language predisposes its speakers to attend to certain aspects of reality as necessary

REFERENCES

Aarsleff, Hans (1982). *From Locke to Saussure: Essays on the Study of Language and Intellectual History*. Minneapolis: University of Minneapolis Press.
Ahluwalia, A. (1978). An Intra-Cultural Investigation of Susceptibility to 'Perspective' and 'Non-Perspective' Spatial Illusions. *British Journal of Psychology* 69 (2): 233–341.
Ahmed-Chamanga, Mohamed (1992). *Lexique Comorien (shindzuani)-Français*. Paris: L'Harmattan.
Algeo, John (2001). A Notable Theosophist: Benjamin Lee Whorf. *Quest* 89 (4): 148–149.
Andrews, B. R. (1903). Habit. *The American Journal of Psychology* 14: 121–149.
Aristotle (1952a). *Rhetoric*. In: W. D. Ross (ed.), *The Works of Aristotle*, Vol. 11. Oxford: Clarendon Press.
Aristotle (1952b). *Poetics*. In: W. D. Ross (ed.), *The Works of Aristotle*, Vol. 11. Oxford: Clarendon Press.
Arnauld, Antoine and Lancelot, Claude (1966). *Grammaire générale et raisonnée, ou La Grammaire de Port-Royal*, présentée par Herbert E. Brekle. Stuttgart-Bad Cannstatt: Frommann.
Arnheim, Rudolf (1969). *Visual Thinking*. Berkeley: University of California Press.
Asch, Solomon (1950). On the Use of Metaphor in the Description of Persons. In: H. Werner (ed.), *On Expressive Language*, pp. 29–39. Worcester: Clark University Press.
Asch, Solomon (1958). The Metaphor: A Psychological Inquiry. In: R. Tagiuri and L. Petrullo (eds.), *Person Perception and Interpersonal Behavior*, pp. 28–42. Stanford: Stanford University Press.
Au, Terrence Kit-Fong (1984). Counterfactuals: In Reply to Bloom. *Cognition* 17: 289–302.
Auster, Paul (2007). Foreword. In: Esther Allen (ed.), *To Be Translated or Not to Be*. Barcelona: Institut Ramon Llul.

Austin, J. L. (1962). *How to Do Things with Words*. Cambridge, MA: Harvard University Press.
Bain, Alexander (1855). *The Senses and the Intellect*. London: Longmans.
Bakhtin, Mikhail M. (1981). *The Dialogic Imagination*. Austin: University of Texas Press.
Bakhtin, Mikhail M. (1986). *Speech Genres and Other Late Essays*, trans. by V. W. McGee, ed. by C. Emerson and M. Holquist. Austin: University of Texas Press.
Bakhtin, Mikhail M. and Voloshinov, Valentin N. (1986). *Marxism and the Philosophy of Language*. Cambridge, MA: Harvard University Press.
Bar–Hillel, Yehoshua (1960). The Present Status of Automatic Translation of Languages. *Advances in Computers* 1: 91–163.
Barnes, John A. (1961). Physical and Social Kinship. *Philosophy of Science* 28 (3): 296–299.
Barthes, Roland (1977). *Image Music Text*. London: Fontana.
Basso, Keith H. (1993). Western Apache Language and Culture: Essays in Linguistic Anthropology. *American Ethnologist*, 20 (1): 195–196.
Bates, Marjory (1923). A Study of the Müller-Lyer Illusion, with Special Reference to Paradoxical Movement and the Effect of Attitude. *The American Journal of Psychology* 34 (1): 46–72.
Bergen, Benjamin (2001). Nativization Processes in L1 Esperanto. *Journal of Child Language* 28 (3): 575–595.
Bergin, Thomas G. and Fisch, Max (1984). *The New Science of Giambattista Vico*. Ithaca: Cornell University Press.
Bergman, Jerry (2011). Benjamin Lee Whorf: An Early Supporter of Creationism. *Acts & Facts* 40 (10): 12–14.
Berlin, Brent and Berlin, Elois A. (1975). Aguarana Color Categories. *American Ethnologist* 2: 61–87.
Berlin, Brent and Kay, Paul (1969). *Basic Color Terms: Their Universality and Evolution*. Berkeley: University of California Press.
Berry, J. W. (1968). Ecology, Perceptual Development and the Müller-Lyer Illusion. *British Journal of Psychology* 59: 205–210.
Betz, John R. (2009). *After Enlightenment: The Post-Secular Vision of J. G. Hamann*. Oxford: Wiley-Blackwell.
Biggam, Carole P. and Kay, Christian (eds.) (2006). *Progress in Colour Studies*. Amsterdam: John Benjamins.
Black, Max (1959). Linguistic Relativity: The Views of Benjamin Lee Whorf. *The Philosophical Review* 68 (2): 228–238.
Black, Max (1962). *Models and Metaphors*. Ithaca: Cornell University Press.
Bloom, Alfred H. (1981). *The Linguistic Shaping of Thought: A Study in the Impact of Language on Thinking in China and the West*. Hillsdale, NJ: Lawrence Erlbaum Associates.
Bloomfield, Leonard (1933). *Language*. New York: Holt.
Boas, Franz (1911). *Handbook of American Indian Languages*. Washington: Bureau of American Ethnology.
Boas, Franz (1920). The Methods of Ethnology. *American Anthropologist* 22: 311–322.
Boas, Franz (1940). *Race, Language, and Culture*. New York: Free Press.
Boas, Franz (1945). *Race and Democratic Society*. New York: J. J. Augustin.
Boas, Franz (1963). *The Mind of Primitive Man*. New York: Collier Books.

Bolinger, Dwight (1968). *Aspects of Language*. New York: Harcourt, Brace, Jovanovich.
Booth, Andrew D. (1955). Use of a Computing Machine as a Mechanical Dictionary. *Nature* 176: 565.
Booth, Andrew D. and Locke, William N. (1955). Historical Introduction. In: W. N. Locke and A. D. Booth (eds.), *Machine Translation of Languages*, pp. 1–14. New York: John Wiley.
Bor, Daniel (2012). *The Ravenous Brain: How the New Science of Consciousness Explains Our Insatiable Search for Meaning*. New York: Basic Books.
Bornstein, Marc H. (2006). Hue Categorization and Color Naming: Physics to Sensation to Perception. In: N. J. Pitchford, and C. P. Biggam (eds.), *Progress in Colour Studies*, pp. 35–68. Amsterdam: John Benjamins.
Bornstein, Marc H., Kessen, William, and Weiskopf, Sally (1976). The Categories of Hue in Infancy. *Science* 191: 201–202.
Boroditsky, Lera (2000). Metaphoric Structuring: Understanding Time through Spatial Metaphors. *Cognition* 75 (1): 1–28.
Boroditsky, Lera (2001). Does Language Shape Thought? Mandarin and English Speakers' Conceptions of Time. *Cognitive Psychology* 43 (1): 1–22.
Boroditsky, Lera (2003). Linguistic Relativity. In: L. Nadel (ed.), *Encyclopedia of Cognitive Science*, pp. 917–922. London: Macmillan.
Boroditsky, Lera (2009). How Does Our Language Shape the Way We Think? *Edge*. https://www.edge.org/conversation/lera_boroditsky-how-does-our-language-shape-the-way-we-think.
Boroditsky, Lera and Ramscar, Michael (2002). The Roles of Body and Mind in Abstract Thought. *Psychological Science* 13 (2): 185–188.
Boroditsky, Lera, Schmidt, Lauren A., and Phillips, Webb (2003). Sex, Syntax, and Semantics. In: D. Gentner, and S. Goldin-Meadow (eds.), *Language in Mind: Advances in the Study of Language and Thought*, pp. 61–80. Cambridge, MA: MIT Press.
Bouton, Mark E. (2007). *Learning and Behavior: A Contemporary Synthesis*. Sinauer: Sunderland.
Bowerman, Melissa (1973). *Early Syntactic Development: A Cross-Linguistic Study with Special Reference to Finnish*. Cambridge: Cambridge University Press.
Brown, Amanda and Gullberg, Marianne (2011). Bidirectional Cross-Linguistic Influence in Event Conceptualization: Expressions of Path among Japanese Learners of English. *Bilingualism: Language and Cognition* 14: 79–94.
Brown, James Cooke (1960). Loglan. *Scientific American* 202: 43–63.
Brown, Penelope and Levinson, Stephen C. (1987). *Politeness: Some Universals in Language Usage*. Cambridge: Cambridge University Press.
Brown, Roger (1958). *Words and Things: An Introduction to Language*. New York: The Free Press.
Brown, Roger (1970). *Psycholinguistics*. New York: The Free Press.
Brown, Roger (1976). In Memorial Tribute to Eric Lenneberg. *Cognition* 4 (2): 125–153.
Brown, Roger, Black, Abraham, and Horowitz, Arnold (1955). Phonetic Symbolism in Natural Languages. *Journal of Abnormal and Social Psychology* (50): 388–393.
Brown, Roger and Lenneberg, Eric (1954). A Study in Language and Cognition. *Journal of Abnormal and Social Psychology* 49 (3): 454–462.

Brugger, Peter and Brugger, Susanne (1993). The Easter Bunny in October: Is It Disguised as a Duck? *Perceptual Motor Skills* 76: 577–578.
Bühler, Karl (1907). Tatsachen und Probleme zu einer Psychologie der Denkvorgänge. Über Gedanken. *Archiv für die gesamte Psychologie* 9 (entire issue).
Butterworth, Brian (1999). *What Counts: How Every Brain is Hardwired for Math.* New York: Free Press.
Candland, Douglas K. (1993). *Feral Children and Clever Animals.* Oxford: Oxford University Press.
Carmichael, L., Hogan, H. P., and Walter, A. A. (1932). An Experimental Study of the Effect of Language on Visually Perceived Form. *Journal of Experimental Psychology* 15: 73–86.
Carr, Nicholas (2011). *The Shallows: What the Internet Is Doing to Our Brains.* New York: Norton.
Carr, Nicholas (2015). *The Glass Cage: How Our Computers Are Changing Us.* New York: Norton.
Carroll, Lewis (1871). *Through the Looking-Glass, and What Alice Found There.* London: Macmillan.
Casarett, David, Pickard, Amy, Fishman, Jessica M., Alexander, Stewart C., Arnold, Robert M., Pollak, Kathryn I., and Tulsky James A. (2010). Can Metaphors and Analogies Improve Communication with Seriously Ill Patients? *Journal of Palliative Medicine* 13: 255–260.
Casasanto, Daniel (2008). Who's Afraid of the Big Bad Whorf? Crosslinguistic Differences in Temporal Language and Thought. *Language Learning* 58 (1): 63–79.
Casasanto, Daniel (2015). Whorfian Hypothesis. *Oxford Bibliographies.* oxfordbibliographies.com/view/document/obo-9780199766567/obo-9780199766567-0058.xml
Cassirer, Ernst A. (1946). *Language and Myth.* New York: Dover.
Chase, Stuart (1958). *Some Things Worth Knowing.* New York: Harper & Brothers.
Cheng, P. Wenjie (2013). Pictures of Ghosts: A Critique of Alfred Bloom's The Linguistic Shaping of Thought. *American Anthropologist* 87 (4): 917–922.
Chomsky, Noam (1957). *Syntactic Structures.* The Hague: Mouton.
Chomsky, Noam (1965). *Aspects of the Theory of Syntax.* Cambridge, MA: MIT Press.
Chomsky, Noam (1966). *Cartesian Linguistics: A Chapter in the History of Rationalist Thought.* New York: Harper & Row.
Chomsky, Noam (1975). *Reflections on Language.* New York: Pantheon.
Chomsky, Noam (1980). On Cognitive Structures and their Development: A Reply to Piaget. In: M. Piattelli-Palmarini (ed.), *Language and Learning: The Debate Between Jean Piaget and Noam Chomsky.* Cambridge: Harvard University Press.
Chomsky, Noam (1986). *Knowledge of Language.* Westport: Praeger.
Christie, Stella and Gentner, Dedre (2012). Language and Cognition in Development. In: M. M. Spivey, K. McRae, and M. Joanisse (eds.), *The Cambridge Handbook of Psycholinguistics.* Cambridge: Cambridge University Press.
Cibelli, Emily, Xu, Yang, Austerweil, Joseph L., Griffiths, Thomas L., and Regier, Terry (2016). The Sapir-Whorf Hypothesis and Probabilistic Inference: Evidence from the Domain of Color. *PLOS ONE.* 11 (7): e0158725.
Classen, Constance (1991). The Sensory Order of Wild Children. In: David Howes (ed.), *The Varieties of Sensory Experience*, pp. 47–60. Toronto: University of Toronto Press.

Cole, K. C. (1984). *Sympathetic Vibrations*. New York: Bantam.
Coleman, E. Gabriella (2010). Ethnographic Approaches to Digital Media. *Annual Review of Anthropology* 39: 487–505.
Comrie, Bernard (1984). Review of Ekkehart Malotki, Hopi Time. *Australian Journal of Linguistics* 4: 131–133.
Comrie, Bernard (1985). *Tense*. Cambridge: Cambridge University Press.
Conklin, Harold (1955). Hanonóo Color Categories. *Southwestern Journal of Anthropology* 11: 339–344.
Coseriu, Eugenio (1973). *Probleme der strukturellen Semantik*, Vol. 40. Tuebingen: Tuebinger Beitraege zur Linguistik.
Cowie, Fiona (1999). *What's Within? Nativism Reconsidered*. Oxford: Oxford University Press.
Crocker, Charlie (2007). *Lost in Translation: Misadventures in English Abroad*. London: Michael Omara.
Crocker, Charlie (2015). *Utterly Lost in Translation: Even More Misadventures in English Abroad*. London: John Blake.
Crystal, David (1987). *The Cambridge Encyclopedia of Language*. Cambridge: Cambridge University Press.
Crystal, David (2006). *Language and the Internet*. Cambridge: Cambridge University Press.
Curtiss, Susan (1977). *Genie: A Psycholinguistic Study of a Modern-day "Wild Child"*. New York: Academic.
Damasio, Antonio R. (1994). *Descartes' Error: Emotion, Reason, and the Human Brain*. New York: G. P. Putnam's.
Danesi, Marcel (1993). *Vico, Metaphor, and the Origin of Language*. Bloomington: Indiana University Press.
Danesi, Marcel (2003). *Second Language Teaching: A View from the Right Side of the Brain*. Dordrecht: Kluwer.
Danesi, Marcel (2016a). *Language and Mathematics: An Interdisciplinary Approach*. Berlin: Mouton de Gruyter.
Danesi, Marcel (2016b). *The Semiotics of Emoji: The Rise of Visual Language in the Age of the Internet*. London: Bloomsbury.
Danesi, Marcel (2017a). *Conceptual Fluency Theory and the Teaching of Foreign Languages*. New York: Nova Science Publishers.
Danesi, Marcel (2017b). The Bidirectionality of Metaphor. *Poetics Today* 38: 15–33.
Danesi, Marcel (ed.) (2019). *Interdisciplinary Perspectives on Math Cognition*. New York: Springer.
Danesi, Marcel (2020). *The Quest for Meaning: A Guide to Semiotic Theory and Practice*, 2nd ed. Toronto: University of Toronto Press.
Danesi, Marcel and Maida-Nicol, Sara (eds.) (2012). *Foundational Texts in Linguistic Anthropology*. Toronto: Canadian Scholars Press.
Danesi, Marcel and Rocci, Andrea (2009). *Global Linguistics: An Introduction*. Berlin: Mouton de Gruyter.
Darnell, Regna (1990). *Edward Sapir: Linguist, Anthropologist, Humanist*. Berkeley: University of California Press.
Deacon, Terrence W. (1997). *The Symbolic Species: The Co-Evolution of Language and the Human Brain*. Harmondsworth: Penguin.
Derks, Lucas and Hollander, Jaap (1996). *Essenties van NLP*. Utrecht: Servire.
Deutscher, Guy (2010). *Through the Language Glass: Why the World Looks Different in Other Languages*. New York: Picador.

Dineen, Francis P. (1995). *General Linguistics.* Washington, DC: Georgetown University Press.
Dinwoodie, David W. (2006). Time and the Individual in Native North America. In: Sergei Kan, Pauline Turner Strong, and Raymond Fogelson (eds.). *New Perspectives on Native North America: Cultures, Histories, and Representations.* Lincoln: University of Nebraska Press.
Doyle, James A. (1985). *Sex and Gender: The Human Experience.* Iowa: William C. Brown.
Duranti, Alessandro (2003). Language as Culture in U.S. Anthropology: Three Paradigms. *Current Anthropology* 44 (3): 323–348.
Ebbinghaus, Hermann (1885). *Memory: A Contribution to Experimental Psychology.* New York: Columbia University Press.
Edwards, Derek (1991). Categories Are for Talking: On the Cognitive and Discursive Bases of Categorization. *Theory and Psychology* 1: 515–542.
Edwards, Derek (1994). Whorf's Empty Gasoline Drum and the Pope's Missing Wife. *Journal of Pragmatics* 22: 215–218.
Elgin, Suzette Haden and Martin, Diane (1988). *A First Dictionary and Grammar of Láadan.* Madison: Society for the Furtherance and Study of Fantasy and Science Fiction.
Emantian, Michelle (1995). Metaphor and the Expression of Emotion: The Value of Cross-Cultural Perspectives. *Metaphor and Symbolic Activity* 10: 163–182.
Enfield, N. J. (2015). Linguistic Relativity from Reference to Agency. *Annual Review of Anthropology* 44: 207–224.
Euler, Robert C. and Dobyns, Henry F. (1971). *The Hopi People.* Phoenix: Indian Tribal Series.
Evans, Vyvyan (2017). *The Emoji Code: The Linguistics Behind Smiley Faces and Scaredy Cats.* New York: Picador.
Evans-Pritchard, Edward E. (1940). *The Nuer.* Oxford: Oxford University Press.
Everett, Daniel (2005). Cultural Constraints on Grammar and Cognition in Pirahã. *Current Anthropology* 46: 621–624.
Faltz, Leonard M. (1998). *The Navajo Verb.* Albuquerque: University of New Mexico Press.
Fauconnier, Gilles and Turner, Mark (2002). *The Way We Think: Conceptual Blending and the Mind's Hidden Complexities.* New York: Basic.
Finkbeiner, Rita, Meibauer, Jörg, and Schumacher, Petra B. (2012). *What Is a Context? Linguistic Approaches and Challenges.* Amsterdam: John Benjamins.
Fleming, Luke (2012). Gender Indexicality in the Native Americas: Contributions to the Typology of Social Indexicality. *Language in Society* 41: 295–320.
Fodor, Jerry A. (1975). *The Language of Thought.* New York: Crowell.
Foucault, Michel (1966). *Les mots et les choses.* Paris: Gallimard.
Foucault, Michel (1972). *The Archeology of Knowledge,* trans. by A. M. Sheridan Smith. New York: Pantheon.
Fox, Robin (1977). *Kinship and Marriage: An Anthropological Perspective.* Harmondsworth: Penguin.
Frye, Northrop (1981). *The Great Code: The Bible and Literature.* Toronto: Academic Press.
Genova, Dafina (2003). Idealized Cognitive Models and Other Mental Representations. In: D. Ginev (ed.), *Bulgarian Studies in the Philosophy of Science. Boston Studies in the Philosophy of Science,* Vol. 236. Dordrecht: Springer.

Gentner, Dedre (2003). Why We're So Smart. In: D. Gentner and S. Goldin-Meadow (eds.), *Language in Mind: Advances in the Study of Language and Thought*, pp. 195–235. Cambridge, MA: MIT Press.
Gerrand, Peter (2007). Estimating Linguistic Diversity on the Internet: A Taxonomy to Avoid Pitfalls and Paradoxes. *Journal of Computer-Mediated Communication* 12: 1298–1321.
Gibbs, Raymond W. (2017). *Metaphor Wars: Conceptual Metaphors in Human Life*. Cambridge: Cambridge University Press.
Gipper, Helmut (1972). *Gibt es ein sprachliches Relativitätsprinzip? Untersuchungen zur Sapir-Whorf-Hypothese*. Frankfurt am Main: S. Fischer.
Gleason, H. A. (1955). *An Introduction to Descriptive Linguistics*. New York: Henry Holt.
Goddard, Cliff and Wierzbicka, Anna (2002). *Meaning and Universal Grammar: Theory and Empirical Findings*. Amsterdam: John Benjamins.
Goffman, Erving (1959). *The Presentation of Self in Everyday Life*. Garden City: Doubleday.
Gordon, Peter (2004). Numerical Cognition Without Words: Evidence from Amazonia. *Science* 306: 496–499.
Graham, Paul (2010). *Hackers & Painters: Big Ideas from the Computer Age*. Sebastopol: O'Reilly Media.
Greenberg, Joseph H. (1966). *Language Universals*. The Hague: Mouton.
Greenfield, Susan (2015). *Mind Change*. New York: Random House.
Greenway, John (1964). *The Inevitable Americans*. New York: Alfred E. Knopf.
Guhe, Markus, Pease, Alison, Smaill, Alan, Martínez, Maricarmen, Schmidt, Martin, Gust, Helmar, Kühnberger, Kai-Uwe, Krumnack, Ulf (2011). A Computational Account of Conceptual Blending in Basic Mathematics. *Cognitive Systems Research* 12: 249–265.
Gumperz, John J. (1965). The Speech Community. *Encyclopedia of the Social Sciences* 9 (3): 382–386.
Gumperz, John J. and Levinson, Stephen C. (eds.) (1996). *Rethinking Linguistic Relativity*. Cambridge, MA: Cambridge University Press.
Guzman, Andrea L. (ed.) (2018). *Human-Machine Communication: Rethinking Communication, Technology, and Ourselves*. New York: Peter Lang.
Haas, Mary R. (1944). Men's and Women's Speech in Koasati. *Language* 20: 142–149.
Hardin, C. L. and Maffi, Luisa (eds.) (1997). *Color Categories in Thought and Language*. Cambridge: Cambridge University Press.
Harré, Rom (1981). *Great Scientific Experiments*. Oxford: Phaidon Press.
Haviland, John (1996). Projections, Transpositions, and Relativity. In: J. Gumperz and S. Levinson (eds.), *Rethinking Linguistic Relativity*, pp. 271–323. Cambridge, MA: Cambridge University Press.
Haviland, William (2002). *Cultural Anthropology*. Wadsworth.
Hawkins, Jeff and Blakeslee, Sandra (2004). *On Intelligence*. New York: Times Books.
Heisenberg, Werner (1949). *The Physical Principles of Quantum Theory*. New York: Dover.
Helprin, Mark (2009). *Digital Barbarism: A Writer's Manifesto*. New York: HarperCollins.
Herder, Johann Gottfried (1770). *Abhandlungen über den Ursprung der Sprache*. Berlin: Christian Friedrich Voß.

Herder, Johann Gottfried (1772a). *Sprachphilosophische Schriften*. Berlin: Christian Friedrich Voß.
Herder, Johann Gottfried (1772b). *Über den Ursprung der Sprache*. Verlag Freies Geistesleben.
Herodotus (c. 430 BCE). *Historia*, trans. by George Rawlinson. Ware: Wordsworth, n.d.
Heynick, Frank (1983). From Einstein to Whorf: Space, Time, Matter, and Reference Frames in Physical and Linguistic Relativity. *Semiotica* 45: 35–64.
Hjelmslev, Louis (1959). *Essais linguistique*. Copenhagen: Munksgaard.
Hoijer, Harry (ed.) (1954). *Language in Culture: Conference on the Interrelations of Language and Other Aspects of Culture*. Chicago: University of Chicago Press.
Hollan, Douglas (2000). Constructivist Models of Mind, Contemporary Psychoanalysis, and the Development of Culture Theory. *American Anthropologist* 102 (3): 538–550.
Holyoak, Keith J. and Stamenkovic, Dušan (2018). Metaphor Comprehension: A Critical Review of Theories and Evidence. *Pyschological Bulletin* 144: 641–671.
Honeck, Richard P. and Hoffman, Robert R. (eds.) (1980). *Cognition and Figurative Language*. Hillsdale, NJ: Lawrence Erlbaum.
Hubbard Edward M., Arman, A. Cyrus, Ramachandran Vilayanur S., and Boynton, Geoggrey M. (2005). Individual Differences among Grapheme-Color Synesthetes: Brain-Behavior Correlations. *Neuron* 45: 975–985.
Humboldt, Wilhelm von (1836). *On Language: The Diversity of Human Language-Structure and Its Influence on the Mental Development of Mankind*, trans. by P. Heath. Cambridge: Cambridge University Press.
Hutchins, Edwin (1995). *Cognition in the Wild*. Cambridge, MA: MIT Press.
Hyde, Daniel C. (2011). Two Systems of Non-Symbolic Numerical Cognition. *Frontiers in Human Neuroscience*. 10.3389/fnhum.2011.00150.
Hyde, G. M. (1993). The Whorf-Sapir Hypothesis and the Translation Muddle. *Translation and Literature* 2: 3–16.
Hymes, Dell H. (1961). On the Typology of Cognitive Styles in Language (with Examples from Chinookan). *Anthropological Linguistics* 3: 22–54.
Hymes, Dell H. (1963). Toward a History of Linguistic Anthropology. *Anthropological Linguistics* 5 (1): 59–103.
Hymes, Dell H. (1964). *Foundation of Sociolinguistics: An Ethnographic Approach*. Philadelphia, PA: University of Pennsylvania Press.
Hymes, Dell H. (1966). *Two Types of Linguistic Relativity (with Examples from Amerindian Ethnography)*. In: William Bright (ed.), *Sociolinguistics. Proceedings of the UCLA Sociolinguistics Conference*.
Hymes, Dell H. (1971). *On Communicative Competence*. Philadelphia: University of Pennsylvania Press.
Imai, Mutsumi and Gentner, Dedre (1997). A Crosslinguistic Study of Early Word Meaning: Universal Ontology and Linguistic Influence. *Cognition* 62: 169–200.
Iverson, Kenneth E. (1962). *A Programming Language*. New York: Wiley.
Iverson, Kenneth E. (1980). Notation as a Tool of Thought. *Communications of the ACM* 23 (8): 444–465.
James, William (1890). *The Principles of Psychology*. New York: Henry Holt.
Jastrow, Joseph (1899). The Mind's Eye. *Popular Science Monthly* 54: 299–312.
Jespersen, Otto (1922) *Language: Its Nature, Development and Origin*. London: Allen & Unwin.

References

Johnson, Mark (1987). *The Body in the Mind: The Bodily Basis of Meaning, Imagination and Reason*. Chicago: University of Chicago Press.
Jones, Robert (1982). *Physics as Metaphor*. New York: New American Library.
Kadvany, John (2007). Positional Value and Linguistic Recursion. *Journal of Indian Philosophy* 35. 487–520.
Kay, Paul (1975). Synchronic Variability and Diachronic Change in Basic Color Terms. *Language in Society* 4: 257–270.
Kay, Paul and Kempton, Willett (1984). What Is the Sapir-Whorf Hypothesis? *American Anthropologist* 86 (1): 65–79.
Kay, Paul and Maffi, Luisa (1999). Color Appearance and the Emergence and Evolution of Basic Color Lexicons. *American Anthropologist* 101: 743–760.
Kay, Paul and Regier, Terry (2006). Language, Thought and Color: Recent Developments. *Trends in Cognitive Sciences* 10 (2): 51–54.
Kecskes, Istvan (2000). A Cognitive-Pragmatic Approach to Situation-Bound Utterances. *Journal of Pragmatics* 32: 605–625.
Keen, Ian (2014). Language in the Constitution of Kinship. *Anthropological Linguistics* 56: 1–53.
Keller, Reiner (2011). The Sociology of Knowledge Approach to Discourse (SKAD). *Human Studies* 34: 43–65.
Kimball, Geoffrey (1991). *Koasati Grammar*. Lincoln: University of Nebraska Press.
King, Ruth (1991). *Talking Gender: A Nonsexist Guide to Communication*. Toronto: Copp Clark Pitman Ltd.
Koffka, Kurt (1921). *The Growth of the Mind*. London: Routledge & Kegan Paul.
Köhler, Wolfgang (1925). *The Mentality of Apes*. London: Routledge & Kegan Paul.
Korzybski, Alfred (1921). *Manhood of Humanity: The Science and Art of Human Engineering*. New York: Dutton.
Korzybski, Alfred (1933). *Science and Sanity: An Introduction to Non-Aristotelian Systems and General Semantics*. Brooklyn: Institute of General Semantics.
Kövecses, Zoltán (1986). *Metaphors of Anger, Pride, and Love: A Lexical Approach to the Structure of Concepts*. Amsterdam: John Benjamins.
Kövecses, Zoltán (1988). *The Language of Love: The Semantics of Passion in Conversational English*. London: Associated University Presses.
Kövecses, Zoltán (1990). *Emotion Concepts*. New York: Springer.
Kövecses, Zoltán (2008). Conceptual Metaphor Theory: Some Criticisms and Alternative Proposals. *Annual Review of Cognitive Linguistics* 6: 168–184.
Kövecses, Zoltán (2010). *Metaphor: A Practical Introduction*. Oxford: Oxford University Press.
Kövecses, Zoltán (2020). *Extended Conceptual Metaphor Theory*. Cambridge: Cambridge University Press.
Kramsch, Claire (1998). *Language and Culture*. Oxford: Oxford University Press.
Kristeva, Julia (1980). *Desire in Language: A Semiotic Approach to Literature and Art*. New York: Columbia University Press.
Kuhn, Thomas S. (1970). *The Structure of Scientific Revolutions*. Chicago: University of Chicago Press.
Kulick, Don (1992). *Language Shift and Cultural Reproduction: Socialization, Self and Syncretism in a Papua New Guinea Village*. Cambridge: Cambridge University Press.

References

Kurzweil, Ray (1999). *The Age of Spiritual Machines*. New York: Viking Press.
Kurzweil, Ray (2005). *The Singularity Is Near*. Harmondsworth: Penguin.
Kurzweil, Ray (2012). *How to Create a Mind: The Secret of Human Thought Revealed*. New York: Viking.
Lakoff, George (1987). *Women, Fire and Dangerous Things: What Categories Reveal About the Mind*. Chicago: University of Chicago Press.
Lakoff, George (2004). *Don't think of an Elephant!: Know Your Values and Frame the Debate*. White River Junction, VT: Chelsea Green.
Lakoff, George (2011). What Scientific Concept Would Improve Everybody's Cognitive Toolkit? *Edge*. https://www.edge.org/response-detail/10093.
Lakoff, George (2012). The Contemporary Theory of Metaphor. In: Marcel Danesi and Sara Maida–Nicol (eds.), *Foundational Texts in Linguistic Anthropology*, pp. 128–171. Toronto: Canadian Scholars' Press.
Lakoff, George and Johnson, Mark (1980). *Metaphors We Live By*. Chicago: Chicago University Press.
Lakoff, George and Johnson, Mark (1999). *Philosophy in the Flesh*. New York: Basic Books.
Lakoff, George and Núñez, Rafael (2000). *Where Mathematics Comes From: How the Embodied Mind Brings Mathematics into Being*. New York: Basic Books.
Lakoff, Robin (1975). *Language and Woman's Place*. New York: Harper & Row.
Lang, Sonja (2014). *Toki Pona: The Language of Good*. Dakha: Tawhid.
Langacker, Ronald W. (1987). *Foundations of Cognitive Grammar*. Stanford: Stanford University Press.
Langacker, Ronald W. (1988). An Overview of Cognitive Linguistics. In: B. Rudzka–Ostyn (ed.), *Topics in Cognitive Linguistics*, pp. 3–48. Amsterdam: John Benjamins.
Langacker, Ronald W. (1990). *Concept, Image, and Symbol: The Cognitive Basis of Grammar*. Berlin: Mouton de Gruyter.
Langacker, Ronald W. (1999). *Grammar and Conceptualization*. Berlin: Mouton de Gruyter.
Langham, James W. (2009). *Humboldt, Worldview and Language*. Edinburgh: Edinburgh University Press.
Law, Vivien (2003). *The History of Linguistics in Europe from Plato to 1600*. Cambridge: Cambridge University Press.
Leavitt, John (2011). *Linguistic Relativities: Language Diversity and Modern Thought*. Cambridge: Cambridge University Press.
Lee, Penny (1991). Whorf's Hopi Tensors: Subtle Articulators in the Language/Thought Nexus? *Cognitive Linguistics* 2 (2): 123–148.
Lee, Penny (1996). *The Whorf Theory Complex: A Critical Reconstruction*. Amsterdam: John Benjamins.
Leibniz, Gottfried Wilhelm (1714). *La monadologie*. Paris: E. Boutroux.
Lenneberg, Eric (1953). Cognition in Ethnolinguistics. *Language* 29: 463–471.
Lenneberg, Eric and Roberts, John (1953). *The Denotata of Language Terms*. Paper presented at the Linguistic Society of America, Bloomington, IN.
Lévi-Strauss, Claude (1958). *Anthropologie structurale*. Paris: Plon.
Lévi-Strauss, Claude (1962). *La pensée sauvage*. Paris: Plon.
Levine, Robert (1997). *A Geography of Time: The Temporal Misadventures of a Social Psychologist or How Every Culture Keeps Time Just a Little Bit Differently*. New York: Basic Books.

Levinson, Stephen C. (1996). Language and Space. *Annual Review of Anthropology* 25: 353–382.
Levinson, Stephen C. (2000). Yélî Dnye and the Theory of Basic Color Terms. *Journal of Linguistic Anthropology* 10: 3–55.
Levinson, Stephen C. and Brown, Penelope (1994). Immanuel Kant among the Tenejapans: Anthropology as Empirical Philosophy. *Ethos* 22 (1): 3–41.
Levinson, Stephen C. and Jaisson, Pierre (2006). *Evolution and Culture*. Cambridge, MA: MIT Press.
Levinson, Stephen C. and Wilkins, David P. (2006). *Grammars of Space*. Cambridge: Cambridge University Press.
Levy, Robert I. (1973). *Tahitians: Mind and Experience in the Society Islands*. Chicago: University of Chicago.
Locke, John (1690). *An Essay Concerning Humane Understanding*, ed. by P. H. Nidditch. Oxford: Clarendon Press.
Lotman, Yuri (1991). *Universe of the Mind: A Semiotic Theory of Culture*. Bloomington: Indiana University Press.
Lowie, Robert H. (1917). *Culture and Ethnology*. Whiefish, Montana: Kessinger.
Lucy, John A. (1985). The Historical Relativity of the Linguistic Relativity Hypothesis. *Quarterly Newsletter of the Laboratory of Comparative Human Cognition* 7: 103–108.
Lucy, John A. (1992a). *Grammatical Categories and Cognition: A Case Study of the Linguistic Relativity Hypothesis*. Cambridge: Cambridge University Press.
Lucy, John A. (1992b), *Language Diversity and Thought: A Reformulation of the Linguistic Relativity Hypothesis*. Cambridge: Cambridge University Press.
Lucy, John A. (1996). The Scope of Linguistic Relativity: An Analysis and Review of Empirical Research. In: J. Gumperz and S. C. Levinson (eds.). *Rethinking Linguistic Relativity*, pp. 37–69. Cambridge, MA: Cambridge University Press.
Lucy, John A. (1997a). Linguistic Relativity. *Annual Review of Anthropology* 26: 291–312.
Lucy, John A. (1997b). The Linguistics of "Color". In: C. L. Hardin and L. Maffi (eds.), *Color Categories in Thought and Language*, pp. 320–346. Cambridge: Cambridge University Press.
Lucy, John A. (2001). Sapir-Whorf Hypothesis. In: *International Encyclopedia of the Social & Behavioral Sciences*, pp. 903–906. Oxford: Elsevier.
Lucy, John A. (2014). Methodological Approaches in the Study of Linguistic Relativity. In: Luna Filipović and Martin PÜtz (eds.), *Multilingual Cognition and Language Use: Processing and Typological Perspectives*, pp. 17–44. Amsterdam: John Benjamins.
Lucy, John A. and Gaskins, Suzanne (2003) Interaction of Language Type and Referent Type in the Development of Nonverbal Classification Preferences. In: D. Gentner and S. Goldin-Meadow (eds.), *Language in Mind: Advances in the Study of Language and Thought*, pp. 465–492. Cambridge, MA: MIT Press.
Lucy, John and Gaskins, Suzanne (2001). Grammatical Categories and the Development of Classification Preferences: A Comparative Approach. In: M. Bowerman and S. Levinson (eds.), *Language Acquisition and Conceptual Development*, pp. 257–283. Cambridge: Cambridge University Press.
Ludden, David (2015). Fifty Shades of Grue: The Intimate Relationship Between Language and Color Perception. *Psychology Today* .psychologytoday.com/us/blog/talking-apes/201502/fifty-shades-grue.

MacCormac, Eric (1985). *A Cognitive Theory of Metaphor*. Cambridge, MA: MIT Press.
MacLaury, Robert (1989). Zapotec Body-Part Locatives: Prototypes and Metaphoric Extensions. *International Journal of American Linguistics* 55: 119–154.
Magnus, Margaret (1999). *Gods of the Word: Archetypes in the Consonants*. Kirksville, MI: Thomas Jefferson University Press.
Malinowski, Bronislaw (1922). *Argonauts of the Western Pacific*. New York: Dutton.
Malotki, Ekkehart (1983). *Hopi Time: A Linguistic Analysis of the Temporal Concepts in the Hopi Language*. Berlin: Mouton.
Mariotto, A. (2010). Hypocognition and Evidence-Based Medicine. *Internal Medicine Journal* 40 (1): 80–82.
Martin, James M. (1990). *A Computational Model of Metaphor Interpretation*. Boston: Academic.
Martin, Laura (1986). Eskimo Words for Snow: A Case Study in the Genesis and Decay of an Anthropological Example. *American Anthropologist* 88: 418–423.
Mathiot, Madeleine (1962). Noun Classes and Folk Taxonomy in Papago. *American Anthropologist* 64: 340–350.
Mathiot, Madaleine (ed.) (1979). *Ethnolinguistics: Boas, Sapir and Whorf Revisited*. The Hague: Mouton.
Maturana, Humberto and Varela, Francisco (1973). *Autopoiesis and Cognition: The Realization of the Living*. Dordrecht: Reidel.
McComiskey, Bruce (2002). *Gorgias and the New Sophistic Rhetoric*. Carbondale: Southern Illinois University Press.
McLuhan, Marshall (1962). *The Gutenberg Galaxy: The Making of Typographic Man*. Toronto: University of Toronto Press.
McLuhan, Marshall (1964). *Understanding Media: The Extensions of Man*. Cambridge: MIT Press.
McNeill, David (1992). *Hand and Mind: What Gestures Reveal about Thought*. Chicago: University of Chicago Press.
McWhorter, John (2009). *Our Magnificent Bastard Tongue: The Untold History of English*. Harmondsworth: Penguin.
McWhorter, John (2016). *The Language Hoax: Why the World Looks the Same in Any Language*. Oxford: Oxford University Press.
Mettrie, Jacques de la (1748). *L'homme machine*. Leyde: Elie Luzac.
Mill, James (1829). *Analysis of the Phenomena of the Human Mind*. London: Longmans.
Miller, Casey and Swift, Kate (1971). *Words and Women*. New York: Harper & Row.
Miller, Casey and Swift, Kate (1988). *The Handbook of Nonsexist Writing*. New York: Harper & Row.
Miller, Robert L. (1968). *The Linguistic Relativity Principle and Humboldtian Ethnolinguistics: A History and Appraisal*. The Hague: Mouton.
Minkowski, Hermann (1909). *Space and Time: Minkowski's Papers on Relativity*. Montreal: Minkowski Institute Press.
Montague, Richard (1974). *Formal Philosophy: Selected Papers of Richard Montague*. New Haven: Yale University Press.
Morgan, Lewis Henry (1871). *Systems of Consanguinity and Affinity of the Human Family*. Washington: Smithsonian.
Müller-Lyer, Franz Carl (1889). Optische Urteilstäuschunge. *Archiv für Physiologie Suppl*: 263–270.

Müller, Friedrich Max (1864). *The Science of Thought*. London: Longmans, Green & Co.
Nainggolan, Flora (2014). Language and Culture: Kinship System of Batak Toba-Samosir Ethnic. *GSTF Journal of Education* 2: http://dl6.globalstf.org/index.php/jed/article/view/681
Neuman, Yair (2014). *Introduction to Computational Cultural Psychology*. Cambridge: Cambridge University Press.
Newton, Sir Isaac (1704). *Opticks*. London: William Innys.
Niemeier, Susanne and Dirven, René (eds.) (1997). *Evidence for Linguistic Relativity*. Amsterdam: John Benjamins.
Ninio, Jacques (2014). Geometrical Illusions Are Not Always Where You Think They Are: A Review of Some Classical and Less Classical Illusions, and Ways to Describe Them. *Frontiers in Human Neuroscience* 8: 10.3389/fnhum.2014.00856.
Ochs, Elinor and Schieffelin, Bambi B. (1984). Language Acquisition and Socialization: Three Developmental Stories and their Implications. In: Richard Shweder and Robert A. LeVine (eds.), *Culture Theory: Essays on Mind, Self, and Emotion*, pp. 276–320. Cambridge: Cambridge University Press.
Ochs, Elinor and Taylor, Carolyn (2001). The Father Knows Best Dynamic in Dinnertime Narratives. In: Alessandro Duranti (ed.), *Linguistic Anthropology: A Reader*, pp. 431–449. Oxford: Blackwell.
Ogden, Charles (1932). *Opposition: A Linguistic and Psychological Analysis*. London: Paul, Trench, & Trubner.
Okrent, Arika (2009). *In the Land of Invented Languages: Esperanto Rock Stars, Klingon Poets, Loglan Lovers, and the Mad Dreamers Who Tried to Build A Perfect Language*. New York: Spiegel & Grau.
Ollongren, Alexander (2012). *Astrolinguistics: Design of a Linguistic System for Interstellar Communication Based on Logic*. New York: Springer.
Ong, Walter (1982). *Orality and Literacy*. New York: Methuen.
Ortony, Andrew (ed.) (1979). *Metaphor and Thought*. Cambridge: Cambridge University Press.
Orwell, George (1949) *1984*. New York: Harcourt Brace.
Parsons, John Herbert (1927). *An Introduction to the Theory of Perception*. Cambridge: Cambridge University Press.
Pavlenko, Aneta (2005). Bilingualism and Thought. In: J. F. Kroll and A. M. DeGroot (eds.), *Handbook of Bilingualism: Psycholinguistic Approaches*, pp. 433–435. Oxford: Oxford University Press.
Pavlov, Ivan (1902). *The Work of Digestive Glands*. London: Griffin.
Pedersen, Eric (2010). Cognitive Linguistics and Linguistic Relativity. In: *The Oxford Handbook of Cognitive Linguistics*. Oxford: Oxford University Press.
Peirce, Charles S. (1931–1958). *Collected Papers*. Cambridge, MA: Harvard University Press.
Piaget, Jean (1969). *The Child's Conception of the World*. Totowa, NJ: Littlefield, Adams & Co.
Piaget, Jean and Inhelder, Barbel (1969). *The Psychology of the Child*. New York: Basic Books.
Pinker, Steven (1994). *The Language Instinct: How the Mind Creates Language*. New York: Harper Perennial.
Pinker, Steven (2007). *The Stuff of Thought: Language as a Window into Human Nature*. New York: Viking.

Pitchford, Nicola J. and Mullen, Kathy T. (2006). The Developmental Acquisition of Basic Colour Terms. In: N. J. Pitchford, and C. P. Biggam (eds.), *Progress in Colour Studies*, pp. 139–158. Amsterdam: John Benjamins.
Plato (2013). *Cratylus*, trans. by Benjamin Jowett. Project Gutenberg. http://www.gutenberg.org/files/1616/1616-h/1616-h.htm.
Pollio, Howard R., Barlow, Jack M., Fine, Harold J., and Pollio, Marilyn R. (1977). *The Poetics of Growth: Figurative Language in Psychology, Psychotherapy, and Education*. Hillsdale, NJ: Lawrence Erlbaum.
Pottier, Bernard (1974). *Linguistique générale*. Paris: Klincksieck.
Prentice, W. C. H. (1954). Visual Recognition of Verbally Labeled Figures. *The American Journal of Psychology* 67 (2): 315–320.
Prince, Alan and Smolensky, Paul (2004). *Optimality Theory: Constraint Interaction in Generative Grammar*. Oxford: Blackwell.
Pula, Robert (1992). The Nietzsche-Korzybski-Sapir-Whorf Hypothesis? *ETC: Review of General Semantics* 49 (1): 50–57.
Pullum, Geoffrey K. (1991). *The Great Eskimo Vocabulary Hoax and other Irreverent Essays on the Study of Language*. Chicago: University of Chicago Press.
Pullum, Geoffrey K. and Scholz, Barbara C. (2002). Empirical Assessment of Stimulus Poverty Arguments. *Linguistic Review* 19: 9–50.
Pütz, Martin and Verspoor, Marjolyn (eds.) (2000). *Explorations in Linguistic Relativity*. Amsterdam: John Benjamins.
Quijada, John (2011). *A Grammar of the Ithkuil Language*. Standard Copyright License.
Ray, Verne (1953). Human Color Perception and Behavioral Response. *Transactions of the New York Academy of Sciences*, 16 (2), Series II, December, pp. 98–104. 10.1111/j.2164-0947.1953.tb01327.x.
Regier, Terry, Kay, Paul, Gilbert, Audrey L., and Ivry, Richard B. (2010). Language and Thought: Which Side Are You on Anyway? In: Barbara Malt and Phillip Wolff (eds.), *Words and the Mind: How Words Capture Human Experience*. Oxford: Oxford University Press.
Reines, Maria Francisca and Prinze, Jesse (2009). Reviving Whorf: The Return of Linguistic Relativity. *Philosophy Compass* 4 (6): 1022–1032.
Rieux, Jacques and Rollin, Bernard E. 1975. *General and Rational Grammar: The Port–Royal Grammar*. The Hague: Mouton.
Robins, Robert H. (1967). *A Short History of Linguistics*. London: Longman.
Robinson, Andrew (2015). *Einstein: A Hundred Years of Relativity*. Princeton: Princeton University Press.
Rosch, Eleanor (1975). Cognitive Reference Points. *Cognitive Psychology* 7: 532–547.
Russell, Bertrand (1921). *The Analysis of Mind*. London: George Allen & Unwin.
Russell, Peter (1983). *The Global Brain*. New York: Tarcher.
Sapir, Edward (1921). *Language*. New York: Harcourt, Brace, and World.
Sapir, Edward (1929). The Status of Linguistics as a Science. *Language* 5: 207–214.
Sapir, Edward and Swadesh, Morris (1946). American Indian Grammatical Categories. *Word* 2: 103–112.
Saunders, Barbara (1995). Disinterring Basic Color Terms: A Study in the Mystique of Cognitivism. *History of the Human Sciences* 8 (7): 19–38.
Saunders, Barbara, Brakel, Jaap van (1997). Are There Nontrivial Constraints on Colour Categorization? *Behavioral and Brain Sciences* 20 (2): 167–228.
Saussure, Ferdinand de (1916). *Cours de linguistique générale*. Charles Bally and Albert Sechehaye (eds.). Paris: Payot.

References 153

Schaff, Adam (1973). *Language and Cognition*. New York: McGraw-Hill.
Schuessler, Axel (2007). *ABC Etymological Dictionary of Old Chinese*. Honolulu: University of Hawaii Press.
Schwieter, John W. and Ferreira, Aline (eds.) (2017). *The Handbook of Translation and Cognition*. Wiley-Blackwell.
Searle, John R. (1984). *Minds, Brain, and Science*. Cambridge, MA: Harvard University Press.
Searls, David B. (2001). From Jabberwocky to Genome: Lewis Carroll and Computational Biology. *Journal of Computational Biology* 8: 339-348.
Seuren, Pieter A. M. (1998). *Western Linguistics: An Historical Introduction*. Oxford: Wiley-Blackwell.
Seuren, Pieter A. M. (2013). *From Whorf to Montague: Explorations in the Theory of Language*. Oxford: Oxford University Press.
Shannon, Claude E. (1948). A Mathematical Theory of Communication. *Bell Systems Technical Journal* 27: 379–423.
Sherzer, Joel (1987). A Discourse-Centered Approach to Language and Culture. *American Anthropologist* 89: 295–309.
Shi-Xu (2005) *A Cultural Approach to Discourse*. New York: Palgrave.
Shreve, Gregory M. and Angelone, Erik (eds.) (2010). *Translation and Cognition*. Amsterdam: John Benjamins.
Sidnell, Jack (2019). Vietnamese Interlocutor Reference, Linguistic Diversity and Semiotic Mediation. *Paradigmi* 37: 467–490.
Sidnell, Jack and Enfield, N. J. (2012). Language Diversity and Social Action: A Third Locus of Linguistic Relativity. *Current Anthropology* 53: 302–333.
Silverstein, Michael (1976). Shifters, Linguistic Categories, and Cultural Description. In: Keith Basso and Henry A. Selby (eds.), *Meaning in Anthropology*, pp. 11–56, Albuquerque: University of New Mexico Press.
Silverstein, Michael (1979). Language Structure and Linguistic Ideology. In: Paul R. Cline, William Hanks and Carol Hofbauer (eds.), *The Elements: A Parasession on Linguistic Units and Levels*, pp. 193–247. Chicago: Chicago Linguistic Society.
Skemp, Richard R. (1971). *The Psychology of Learning Mathematics*. Harmondsworth: Penguin.
Skinner, B. F. (1938). *The Behavior of Organisms*. New York: Appleton-Century-Crofts.
Slobin Dan I. (1996). From "Thought and Language" to "Thinking for Speaking". In: John Gumperz and Stephen Levinson (eds.), *Rethinking Linguistic Relativity*, pp. 70–96. Cambridge, MA: Cambridge University Press.
Slobin, Dan I. (2003). Language and Thought Online: Cognitive Consequences of Linguistic Relativity. In: D. Gentner, and S. Goldin-Meadow (eds.), *Language in Mind: Advances in the Study of Language and Thought*, pp. 157–192. Cambridge, MA: MIT Press.
Smolin, Lee (2013). *Time Reborn: From the Crisis in Physics to the Future of the Universe*. Boston: Houghton Mifflin Harcourt.
Sontag, Susan (1978). *Illness as Metaphor*. New York: Farrar, Straus & Giroux.
Sontag, Susan (1989). *AIDS and Its Metaphors*. New York: Farrar, Straus & Giroux.
Spitzer, Leo (1928). *Stilstudien*. München: Max Hüber.
Swadesh, Morris (1951). Diffusional Cumulation and Archaic Residue as Historical Explanations. *Southwestern Journal of Anthropology* 7: 1–21.
Swadesh, Morris (1955). Towards Greater Accuracy in Lexicostatistic Dating. *International Journal of American Linguistics* 21: 121–137.

Swadesh, Morris (1959). Linguistics as an Instrument of Prehistory. *Southwestern Journal of Anthropology* 15: 20–35.

Swadesh, Morris (1971). *The Origins and Diversification of Language*. Chicago: Aldine-Atherton.

Swedenborg, Emanuel (1746). *Arcana Coelestia*. New York: Swedenborg Foundation.

Swoyer, Chris (2015). The Linguistic Relativity Hypothesis. *Stanford Encyclopedia of Philosophy*. stanford.library.sydney.edu.au/archives.

Taylor, Douglas M. (1977). *Languages of the West Indies*. Baltimore: Johns Hopkins.

Tenniel, John (2003). *Alice's Adventures in Wonderland and Through the Looking-Glass*. London: Penguin Classics.

Thibodeau PH, Boroditsky L (2013) Natural Language Metaphors Covertly Influence Reasoning. *PLoS ONE* 8(1): e52961. 10.1371/journal.pone.0052961.

Thibodeau P. H., Boroditsky, L. (2015) Measuring Effects of Metaphor in a Dynamic Opinion Landscape. *PLoS ONE* 10(7): e0133939. 10.1371/journal.pone.0133939.

Thompson, E. P. (1967). Time, Work-Discipline and Industrial Capitalism. *Past & Present* 38: 56–97.

Tilley, Christopher (1999). *Metaphor and Material Culture*. Oxford: Blackwell.

Tolman, Edward (1932). *Purposive Behavior in Animals and Men*. New York: Appleton-Century-Crofts.

Tulving, Endel (1972). Episodic and Semantic Memory. In: Endel Tulving and W. Donaldson (eds.), *Organization of Memory*, pp. 23–46. New York: Academic.

Uexküll, Jakob von (1909). *Umwelt und Innenwelt der Tierre*. Berlin: Springer.

Ulam, Stanislas (1958). Tribute to John von Neumann. *Bulletin of the American Mathematical Society* 64: 5.

Underhill, James W. (2011). *Creating Worldviews: Metaphor, Ideology and Language*. Edinburgh: Edinburgh University Press.

Underhill, James W. (2012). *Ethnolinguistics and Cultural Concepts: Truth, Love, Hate and War*. Cambridge: Cambridge University Press.

Vermeulen, Han F. (2015). *Before Boas: The Genesis of Ethnography and Ethnology in the German Enlightenment*. Lincoln: University of Nebraska Press.

Vinge, Vernor (1993). The Coming Technological Singularity: How to Survive in the Post-Human Era. In: G. A. Landis (ed.), *Vision-21: Interdisciplinary Science and Engineering in the Era of Cyberspace*, pp. 11–22. NASA Publication CP-10129.

Vygotsky, Lev S. (1931). *Storia dello sviluppo delle funzioni psichiche superiori*. Firenze: Giunti–Barbèra.

Vygotsky, Lev S. (1962). *Thought and Language*. Cambridge: MIT Press.

Vygotsky, Lev S. (1972). An Experimental Study of Concept Formation. In: P. Adams (ed.), *Language in Thinking*, pp. 277–305. Harmondsworth: Penguin.

Vygotsky, Lev S. (1978). *Mind in Society*. Cambridge: Cambridge University Press.

Vygotsky, Lev S. (1984). *Vygotsky's Collected Works, Vol. 2: Problems of General Psychology*. R. Rieber and A. Carton (ed. and trans.). Cambridge, MA: Harvard University Press.

Watson, John B. (1913). Psychology as the Behaviorist Views It. *Psychological Review* 20: 158–177.

Weaver, Warren (1955). Translation. In: W. N. Locke and A. D. Booth (eds.), *Machine Translation of Languages*, pp. 15–23. New York: John Wiley.

Weizenbaum, Joseph (1966). ELIZA—A Computer Program for the Study of Natural Language Communication between Man and Machine. *Communications of the ACM* 9: 36–45.
Wertheimer, Max (1923). Untersuchungen zur Lehre von der Gestalt, II. *Psychologische Forschungen* 4: 301–350.
Wescott, Roger W. (1980). *Sound and Sense.* Lake Bluff, IL.: Jupiter Press.
Westerman, David, Bowman, Nicholas D., and Lachlan, Kenneth L. (2014). *Introduction to Computer Mediated Communication: A Functional Approach.* Dubuque: Kendall-Hunt.
Whorf, Benjamin Lee (1940). Science and Linguistics. *MIT Technology Review* 42: 229–248.
Whorf, Benjamin Lee (1941). The Relation of Habitual Thought to Language. In: Leslie Spier (ed.), *Language, Culture, and Personality: Essays in Memory of Edward Sapir*, pp. 75–93. Menasha: Sapir Memorial Publication Fund.
Whorf, Benjamin Lee (1946). The Hopi Language, Toreva Dialect. In: Harry Hoijer, (ed.), *Linguistic Structures of Native America*, pp. 158–183. New York: Viking Fund.
Whorf, Benjamin Lee (1956). In: John B. Carroll (ed.), *Language, Thought, and Reality.* Cambridge, MA: MIT Press.
Wiener, Norbert (1948). *Cybernetics, or Control and Communication in the Animal and the Machine.* Cambridge, MA: MIT Press.
Wierzbicka, Anna (1996). *Semantics: Primes and Universals.* Oxford: Oxford University Press.
Wierzbicka, Anna (1997). *Understanding Cultures Through Their Key Words.* Oxford: Oxford University Press.
Wierzbicka, Anna (2003). *Cross-Cultural Pragmatics: The Semantics of Human Interaction.* Berlin: Mouton de Gruyter.
Wierzbicka, Anna (2006). The Semantics of Colour: A New Paradigm. In: N. J. Pitchford and C. P. Biggam, (eds.), *Progress in Colour Studies*, pp. 1–24. Amsterdam: John Benjamins.
Winawer, Jonathan, Witthoft, Nathan, Frank, Michael C, Wu, Lisa, Wade, Alex R., Boroditsky, Lera (2007). Russian Blues Reveal Effects of Language on Color Discrimination. *Proceedings of the National Academy of Sciences* 104: 7780–7785.
Wittgenstein, Ludwig (1921). *Tractatus Logico–Philosophicus.* London: Routledge & Kegan Paul.
Wittgenstein, Ludwig (1953). *Philosophical Investigations.* London: Macmillan.
Wolff, Phillip and Holmes, Kevin J. (2011). Linguistic Relativity. *Cognitive Science* 2: 253–265.
Wu, Kaidi and Dunning, David (2018). Hypocognition: Making Sense of the Landscape Beyond One's Conceptual Reach. *Review of General Psychology* 22 (1): 22–25.
Wundt, Wilhelm (1898). Die geometrisch-optischen Tauschungen. *Abhandlungen der Mathematisch-Physischen Klasse der Königlich-Sächsischen Gesellschaft der Wissenschaften* 42: 55–178.
Zöllner, Johann (1860). Ueber eine neue Art von Pseudoskopie und ihre Beziehungen zu den von Plateau und Oppel beschrieben Bewegungsphaenomenen. *Annalen der Physik* 186: 500–525.

INDEX

agglutinative 4, 5, 13, 25, 90, 134
analytic 5, 122, 134
anthropological linguistics 8
anthropology 62, 129
anthropomorphism 109, 110, 117
Apache 110
Aristotle 5, 74
Arnauld, Antoine 6
Arnheim, Rudolf 12, 73
Artificial General Intelligence 124
artificial intelligence (AI) 122–124
asynchronous 119

Bakhtin, Mikhail 36, 80, 81
Bantu 111
Bar-Hillel paradox 92
Bar-Hillel, Yehoshua 92
Barthes, Roland 95
Basque 11
Bassa 64, 68
Basso, Keith 110
Batak Toba 63
Batammaliba 110
Bauplan 127–129
Bedouin 10, 61
behaviorism 74
Berlin, Brent 15, 65–69, 77
bilingualism 75, 91
Black, Max 44, 45
blending 100, 104, 105, 108, 109
Bloom, Alfred 49, 74
Blub Paradox 123
Boas, Franz ix, 7–9, 20, 23–26, 31, 36, 37, 46, 56, 59
Boroditsky, Lera 50, 51
bricolage 82

Brown, James Cooke 125
Brown, Penelope 82
Brown, Roger 10, 27
Butterworth, Brian 61

calque 87–89
Carroll, Lewis 22, 23, 29, 36, 37
Cassirer, Ernst 11
Chagga 111
Chinese 51, 52, 70, 127, 131
Chinook 4
Chomsky, Noam 7, 11, 12, 15, 20, 29, 30, 34, 41, 46, 74
clustering 105, 107, 117
codability 27, 28, 34, 35, 41, 45, 47, 61, 65, 79
cognition 14, 28, 32, 48, 50, 58, 61, 70, 74, 82, 90, 98, 100, 101, 108, 109, 115, 119, 123, 125, 129, 130
cognitive linguistics x, 9, 34, 98–100, 115
collocation 122
color terms 63–69
communicative competence 8, 19, 36, 60
comparison 26, 108, 109, 112
computer-mediated communication (CMC) 118–121, 127, 131
Comrie, Bernard 46
conceptual metaphor 100
conceptual metaphor theory (CMT) 101, 103, 104, 108, 109
Conklin, Harold 65, 69
connotation 101, 132
context 19, 29, 30, 50, 51, 83, 91–93, 100, 102, 104, 119, 125

Index **157**

conversation 80, 81, 84, 88–90, 119
counterfactual 49
creationism 113
Crystal, David 120
cybernetics 128

denotation 84
diachronic 6, 126
dialogue 80, 81
discourse 35, 36, 46, 80–82, 84
discursive relativity 80, 82–85
duck–rabbit illusion 19
Dyirbal 9

Ebbinghaus curve 35
Ebbinghaus, Hermann 35
Egyptian 9
Einstein, Albert 18, 44
Eliza 122
Emergence Hypothesis 67
emoji 120, 121, 132
Esperanto 121, 125, 126
Ethnography 24, 37, 62
ethnology 24
Euclid 130
Evans-Pritchard, E. E. 7, 62
expective 43, 45

feedback 128
feral children 35, 36
fieldwork 8
focal color 66–69
Fodor, Jerry 46
foreign language 90, 94, 96
Foucault, Michel 36
Frye, Northrop 111
fusional 5

Gaskins, Suzanne 51
gender 9, 54, 56, 62, 83, 84, 119
general semantics 1
generative grammar ix
German 9, 45, 76, 85, 91
Gestalt 48, 74, 101
gesticulant 109
gesture 109, 121
Gipper, Helmut 45
global brain 121
Google Translate 92, 93
Gordon, Peter 61

Gorgias 9
Graham, Paul 123
grammar 3–8, 20, 21, 23, 25, 26, 29, 30, 34, 36, 43–45, 47, 50, 70–78, 84–87, 90, 93, 126, 129
grammatical programming (GP) 71, 72
Greek 9, 49

habit 54, 73, 74
habitual thought 54, 73–75, 77, 80, 82, 86, 89
Haden Elgin, Suzette 126
Hamann, Johann Georg 11
Hanunóo 65, 69
Hawaiian 62
Hebrew 86, 113
Herder, Johann Gottfried von 11
Herodotus 9
Hittite 69
Hoijer, Harry 18, 40
Hopi 15, 16, 18, 20, 40–45, 47, 48, 50, 54, 71, 98, 99, 125
Humboldt, Wilhelm von 11, 12, 20, 27, 37, 51
Hymes, Dell 8, 19, 27, 36, 82, 84
hypocognition 129, 130

iconism 53
idealized cognitive model (ICM) 105–108, 110, 113, 115, 117
idiom 30, 87, 122
image schema 101–104, 108, 109, 116
inceptive 18
inflectional 5
innere Sprachform 11, 27
inner speech 28, 29, 123
intertextuality 95, 96
Inuit 17, 20, 24, 46, 47, 56
Inuktitut 46
irony 102, 103, 116
Iroquois 62
isolating 4, 6, 25, 90
Italian 2, 15, 27, 35, 41, 58, 67, 72, 76, 87, 89–91, 94
Ithkuil 125
Iverson, Kenneth E. 123

Jabberwocky 22, 23, 27, 29, 36, 37
Japanese 67, 83, 86
Jastrow, Joseph 19
Johnson, Mark 100–103, 114, 115

Index

Kawi 11
Kay, Paul 15, 65–70, 77
Khaldun, Ibn 10
Kinship 62, 63
Koasati 84
Korzybski, Alfred 1–3, 14, 19
Kramsch, Claire 50
Kurzweil, Ray 124
Kwakiutl 8

Láadan 125
Lakoff, George 9, 48, 84, 99–102, 104, 105, 108–110, 113–115, 130
Lakoff, Robin 81
Lancelot, Claude 6
Langacker, Ronald 34, 71, 72
Lang, Sonja 125
langue 6, 60
Latin
Lee, Penny 18, 48
Leibniz, Gottfried 10
Lenneberg, Eric 27, 28, 64, 65
Lévi-Strauss, Claude 63, 82
Levy, Robert 129
lexeme 3, 4, 8, 13, 16, 17, 27, 30, 39, 45–47, 59, 60, 66, 76, 103
lexical field 53, 60
lexical programming (LP) 63, 71
lexicology 4
lexicon 4, 7–9, 23, 24, 27, 51, 58, 60, 63, 64, 70, 87
lingua franca 121, 126
linguistic anthropology 8, 9
linguistic determinism x, 10, 12, 15, 27, 34
linguistic relativity 9–15, 128–130
linguistic relativity hypothesis (LRH) viii, ix, x, xi, 2–6, 9, 84, 85, 90, 91, 98–100, 115, 121, 129
Locke, John 52
Loglan 126
lógos 5
Lotman, Yuri 112
Lucy, John 12, 26, 33, 34, 46, 47, 50, 51, 69, 82, 83

MacCormac, Eric 123
Machine Translation (MT) 91–94
Magnus, Margaret 82
Malotki, Ekkehart 15, 16, 45, 47, 48, 98
Mandarin 51, 67
Martin, James M. 123

Martin, Laura 17
Mayan 28, 50
McNeill, David 109
McWhorter, John 16, 17, 46
memory 26, 27, 34, 35, 48, 51, 68, 95, 125
mentalese 16, 46, 109
merge 30
Mesoamerican 41
metaphor 47, 51, 57, 69, 71, 90, 98–100, 103, 104, 106–115, 120, 123, 129
metaphrase 86
metonymy 102, 103, 116
Mettrie, Jacques de la 115
Montague, Richard 30
Morgan, Lewis Henry 62
morpheme 3–5, 13, 17, 26, 45, 50, 52, 126
morphology 4, 13
Müller, Friedrich Max 10
Müller, Gerhard Friedrich 24
Müller-Lyer, Franz Carl 32
Müller-Lyer Illusion 32
Multimodality 120
Munsell color system 66

natural language programming (NLP) 122
Navajo 50, 71, 79, 80
netlingo 120
Neumann, John van 124
nomic 43, 45
Nuer 7, 62

onomatopoeia 52
optical illusion 19, 33
Orwell, George 55

Pāṇini 3, 4
Papago 59, 60
parallel postulate 130
parameter 7
paraphrase 12, 18, 26, 27, 38, 41, 46, 47, 49, 76, 79
parole 6, 60
participant observation 24
Pavlov, Ivan 74
Peirce, Charles S. 75
perception 2, 3, 7, 9, 13, 18, 23, 28, 32–35, 48, 53, 55, 58, 61, 62, 64, 65, 68, 70–72, 80, 82–84, 86, 90, 125

Index

phatic communion 81, 82
phoneme 13, 52
phonetic 13, 51, 52, 56
phonology 13
Piaget, Jean 61, 62
Pinker, Steven 16, 46, 108, 109
Plato 9, 29, 51, 80, 105
Port-Royal Circle 6, 7
Port-Royale Grammar 6, 7
Poverty of the Stimulus 29, 30
pragmatics 13
Priscian 6
psychology 13, 31, 34–36, 69, 73, 74, 101, 129
Pullum, Geoffrey 17, 30, 46

Quijada, John 125

Ray, Verne 3, 12, 64
reportive 43, 45
Rosch, Eleanor 68
Russell, Bertrand 42
Russell, Peter 121
Russian 26, 67, 87, 92

Samoan 52
Sanskrit 3, 4
Sapir, Edward viii, ix, 5, 10–12, 15, 18, 20, 23, 25–28, 31, 36, 37, 40–42, 73, 85, 94
Saunders, Barbara 69
Saussure, Ferdinand de 4, 6, 7, 52
Schleyer, Johann Martin 125
Searle, John 127
semantics 4, 13, 47, 83
semiotic relativity 33, 34, 37, 121, 127, 129, 130, 132
Shannon, Claude 93
Shinzwani 58
Shona 64
Singularity 124, 132
Slobin, Dan 82, 85
Socrates 51, 52, 80
Sontag, Susan 113, 114
sound symbolism 51–53
source domain 101
source language 86
spacetime 18, 42, 44, 71
specialized vocabulary 59–62
Spitzer, Leo 36, 80

Standard Average European (SAE) 16, 40, 42–45, 50, 62, 65, 98, 99, 125
sutra 4
Swadesh, Morris 52
Swahili 69
Swedenborg, Emanuel 10
synchronic 6
synchronous 119
synesthesia 98
syntax 3–6, 13, 25, 73, 77
synthetic 5

Tagalog 115
target domain 101
target language 87, 88
tensor 43, 99
Thompson, E. P. 2
Thrax, Dionysius 6
timeless 15, 20, 42, 44, 47
Toki Pona 125
Tolkein, J. R. 127
translation 79, 85–89, 91, 94
Turkish 14

Uexküll, Jakob von 127, 128
Unicode 121
Universal Grammar (UG) 7
Uto-Aztecan 16, 41, 42

Vico, Giambattista 12
Vinge, Vernor 124
Volapük 125
Vygotsky, Lev 23, 28–31, 34, 37, 108, 119

Weaver, Warren 91
Weizenbaum, Joseph 122
Weltanschauung 11, 12
Weltansicht 12
Wescott, Roger 69
Whorf, Benjamin Lee viii, ix–xi, 5, 6, 12, 15–18, 20, 40–47, 53, 55–57, 63, 68, 70, 73, 79, 85, 86, 112, 118–120
Whorfian Hypothesis (WH) 40
Whorfian Scale 41, 45–47, 53, 69, 79, 90, 129
Wiener, Norbert 128
Wierzbicka, Anna 45, 69, 70
Wilkins, John 125
worldview 3, 7, 9, 11, 12, 15, 16, 25, 27, 28, 44, 48, 125, 130

Yélî 67
Yucatec 26, 50, 51

Zamenhof, Ludwik Lejzer 125, 126
Zapotec 110

Zöllner Illusion 33
Zöllner, Johann 33
Zuñi 27, 28, 67

Printed in the United States
by Baker & Taylor Publisher Services